Joanne,

Ho . . .

. . . , James

FATED . . . But I Never Wanted To Be A Teacher
Was initially released on Amazon Kindle where
up to the date of this publication it had received
eleven reviews and rated 4.8 stars

Sue C called it:- " A master piece . . .
written up so well . . . giggling from start to
finish . . . absolutely the best (money) I've spent
in a long time...Thanks"

Axel:- "Cracking entertainment . . .
Brought me right back to my school days.
Mind you . . . I did go to one of the schools
featured in the book!!"

**John R: You should most certainly think
about a follow up to your book** . . .
Clever writing; it gripped me . . . I laughed, I
cried. What a good read."

James Masters

FATED . . . But I Never Wanted To Be A Teacher

Published by CreateSpace 2013

All Rights Reserved

Contents

Foreword

As the title suggests **I never wanted to be a teacher,** but, also, I had never intended to write an autobiographical book either.

I had already written two non fiction books about Sport and my intention had been to try my hand at fiction next, when two of my friends, independently, suggested that I should write a book detailing all of the scrapes and adventures that I had experienced throughout my life.

My immediate reaction was "who on Earth wants to read the "Diary of Dick Chitt?" OK, autobiographies are popular, but only by Pop Stars or International Footballers, Film Stars, etc."

Bob's reply was "What about the James Herriot books then, and all the other 'It shouldn't happen to . . .' books?"

"Besides you're always telling stories, it's something you're good at."

"A big mouth, you mean."

"I didn't say that . . . but if you insist."

So I considered it.

I certainly was good at telling stories.

When the kids that I taught at one school nicknamed me 'Jack'. I thought there must be a celebrity somewhere, that I hadn't heard, of called Jack Masters, but when I delved into it, I found that it stood for Jackanory, because of the stories I was always telling them.

The only difference between 'Jack' and myself was that my stories were all true.

Yes, you might find some of the anecdotes contained in this book hard to believe - but *believe me* they *are* all true. Fact *is* stranger than fiction!

The only liberty I've taken is in changing the names of locations and characters so as not to embarrass or annoy anyone!

I hope you enjoy reading it.

I certainly enjoyed writing it.

Happy Reading,

Chapter 1

Baptism of Fire

Do you believe in Fate?

No - neither do I!

But I still can't explain why, even though I never wanted to be a teacher – and tried to leave twice, I still came back like a boomerang - (or was that a bad penny?).

Even when I *accidently* landed my ideal job, in a school that I loved, I had originally only intended working there for one or two terms.

As it turned out, I eventually worked there for 16 years and would still be there now if bad health hadn't intervened.

BUT, Heaven only knows why I lasted *that* long. If my first School had had anything to do with it, I would have finished there and then.

It was a nightmare!

I only took the position because someone else was given a job at interview that had originally been promised to me, and, in a fit of pique, I put in a very late application to my home Education Authority.

They must have put all the flags out.

I was given the male version of Saint Trinian's: - Harry Mac's

The school was named after the local politician/Prime Minister, Harold MacMillan, but that was its only connection to anything civilised. The School was boys only - 350 of them – 200 with criminal records and most of the others on the police shortlist.

Someone at the Education Committee must have been rubbing their hands with unexpected delight when the last minute plea came in from this gullible college graduate.

Like the St. Trinian's teachers, I don't suppose they expected me to last long. However I did. But after that first three months, I still don't know how!

I'd only been there for three weeks and here I was staring down at the lifeless body in the road outside of Stockton Sports Centre.

The School, being a typical one from the Victorian era, didn't have its own playing fields. The younger kids had to walk to the council fields . . . but the fifth year were treated to a bus journey to the local sports centre.

It wasn't much of a treat, however, for the teacher taking them.

As you would expect, as soon as the double decker arrived, there was a mass scrum; pushing & barging to get on, with all the naughty kids winning out and heading for the upper deck.

Now, in more modern times one teacher wouldn't be allowed to take so many kids, split between two decks, but this was 1972, *and besides,* nothing was ever simple or normal at Harry Mac's.

The kids were shocked when, unexpectedly, I decided to sit upstairs with the 'villains' leaving the small handful of 'no trouble nerds' to sit downstairs.

The ploy worked.
No problems whatsoever from the 'naughty boys'. But, just as the bus turned the corner into Tilery Street, 40 metres from our destination, the nerds got up and started walking down the aisle – ringing the bus' bell as they went.

Despite furious, high decibel, bellowing down the stairwell by me, it continued.

So, the driver decided to take his own action, and SLAMMED on the brakes in an emergency stop.

The front boy hurtled down the aisle, put his arms across his face (fortunately) as his head hit the inside of the windscreen and, amidst a cacophony of screeching brakes, and splintering & shattering glass, went straight through to land in a heap in front of both the bus and the Sports Centre.

I frantically bounded down the stairs in just two leaps, and looked out of the now open windscreen onto the expected carnage in the street.

The lifeless figure moved, stood up, brushed himself down, and expleted
"F*****g Hell, **F*****g Hell**"
Then he panicked and jammed his hand

across his mouth as he saw me glaring down.

"It's OK, son," I said, "I would have said the same myself !"

The boy recovered, only suffering mild shock – with not a scratch on him.

The driver was not so lucky; after surviving a massive tongue lashing from me, he was disciplined by his employers and suspended from duty.

THIS was only my third week at Harry Mac's, I wasn't even officially in my probationary year, as the Education Committee were so keen to get a 'mug' into the School that they offered me employment before the Summer term had ended.

Being a typical student, with an enormous overdraft, I was only too willing to accept.

That Students Union bar bill wasn't going to pay itself !

However I was now beginning to question the sanity of my decision. There was still more than a year to go – anything could happen in that time – a*nd believe me, it did.*

The Sports Centre incident was just a taster.

I taught in three schools 'permanently' during my career; Harry Mac's was for the shortest duration, but Harry knew how to pack 'em in. I had more incidents there than all of the Others put together.

It truly was a Baptism of Fire.

*   *   *   *   *   *

The start of my probationary year proper was pretty mild and insignificant compared to the above. Little did I know, that this was just the lull before the storm. After all, *this was* the Harold MacMillan Secondary School for Young Boys. Incidents like this were commonplace – or that's how it appeared judging by the way the cardschool hardly looked up from their lunchtime game when I told them what had happened. Even if they *had* shown more reaction I probably wouldn't have seen it, however, as their faces were enveloped in a dense cloud of cigarette smoke which perpetually hung over the tiny staffroom at Harry's.

Before retiring on health grounds, I was a PE teacher for twenty years and yet, fatefully it seems, the three worst accidents that I had ever experienced in my professional career came within weeks of each other here. The place still conjures up nightmares for me even though it has now been closed as a secondary school for more than three decades.

This school would have been be an ordeal for any experienced teacher never mind one who had only a few weeks earlier left training college with the fragrant remains of soap still moist behind his ears.

Harry's was set in one of the most deprived areas of Cleveland, a crumbling relic of Victorian ideals that had long been outdated. An austere red brick facade with marble entrance hall that opened up into a square of dingy classrooms running around a small quadrangle that was the pupils only play area. None of the lush playing fields here, that are now commonplace in modern comprehensives.

Three hundred and fifty boys were enrolled at the school and each class was bussed once a week off site; the younger boys to the municipal swimming baths and the older boys weekly to the local sports centre.

The School was surviving against all the odds and so were the staff. There was a distinct lack of enthusiasm about the place from both pupils and eductators alike. There was only a year to go before it was closed for good, and everybody seemed to be treading water.

Not so though for this enthusiastic young whippersnapper, fresh out of college. He was determined to set his stamp on this place and overcome all the adversities; which in reality almost overcame him.

The above related accident may appear exceptionally traumatic, but it fades into insignificance compared to two that followed.

The first of these occurred shortly after returning to School, following the six weeks summer break. Doug Raymond, Head of Maths, and main card-sharp, couldn't believe it when I declared that I couldn't wait to get back because I had been bored during the holidays.

He just groaned "You'll learn" prophetically, as he shook his head, causing an increased cascade of cigarette ash to splatter all over the card table.

At the time I wrote him off as a sceptical, unenthusiastic, old dinosaur, that had passed his sell-by date. A teacher who shouldn't be in the profession because of this lack of commitment and enthusiasm. As time wore on I found myself growing more and more like him, except for one major difference - I never lost my enthusiasm or energy for teaching the kids.

That didn't mean I was a dedicated teacher! I eventually lost my enthusiasm for the teaching profession and the Government, in general - *but never for the kids.*

     *   *   *   *   *   *

When I was at College I attended the 'Social Medicine' lectures with little relish. I did so because I had to accumulate some credit to make up for the lectures that I missed due to self inflicted illnesses. You know, the one that is very common on all college campuses. It normally occurs when the lecture requiring attendance is very early in the morning, and the student has been up partying most of the previous night. At the time I had doubted whether I would ever need most of the information disseminated. Topics ranged from identifying venereal disease, drug misuse, delivering a baby, to epilepsy,

How wrong I was!

It was a boiling hot day in the tiny gym that also doubled for the School assembly hall. The three wheeled piano had been pushed out into the corridor, and the dingy curtains stuffed behind the wallbars to keep them out of the way, so that 3B's basketball lesson could get underway. All of the 'sick, lame & lazy' pupils were watching from their usual safe position, standing on the window ledges behind the wall bars, as there was no room for benches on the minute playing area.

Suddenly a member of red team stopped and shouted

"Sir, Look at 'arry, '- E's doin' 'is nut."

Sure enough, 'arry was. He was holding onto one of the wallbars shaking ferociously, eyes rolled back in their sockets.

"Jeez" I panicked silently, an epileptic fit.

Racking my brain to recall what Ma Gordon had taught me at College, I realised he was in the best position possible; restricted enough so he couldn't move around to injure himself, or anyone else - but if he swallowed his tongue, I was in trouble.

Jeez, I hoped he didn't swallow his tongue.

Fortunately;- he didn't.

Then true to Ma Gordon's text book, after the fit had run itself out, 'arry blacked out and collapsed to the floor – or in this case the window ledge.

That would have been fine, and I would have just left him there to recover if he hadn't then slipped off the window ledge and jammed himself into the tiny six inch gap between ledge and bars. *I know this seems impossible,* but that is just what he did and now I had the problem that he might not be able to breathe, or might choke himself with his own tongue or vomit.

Frantically, I tried pulling at the wallbars but they wouldn't budge.

"Quick, Appleby, run to the woodwork room and get a hammer and large screwdriver to take these bars off."

I sent the class out to shower & change but most of them simply pulled their schoolclothes on over their sweaty and already stinking PE kit and returned to the gym as quickly as they could to witness the spectacle.

Better than any TV soap this - *real life often is*, I only wished that I hadn't been starring in this episode.

After what seemed like decades, Appleby returned with Cliff Thompson the woodwork teacher, to assist. I wasn't sure that I wanted his assistance as he was already minus one finger that he had lopped off during the summer holidays whilst helping a friend chop down some long grass with a sickle, - *and now he had come to help me!*

At that moment, though, I was beyond caring. We had to get 'arry out from behind the wallbars and into a recovery position as soon as possible, and this time Mr. Thompson's assistance was invaluable.

We both worked like maniacs to unscrew and wrench the wall bars from their frame, and then laid Harry on the gym floor in the recovery position. Then we started to loosen his clothing. It was a blistering hot summer's day, and the windows behind the wallbars must have magnified the sun's rays to make it practically unbearable, so I was absolutely staggered to find that Harry was wearing a parka, a jumper, a grey school shirt (or was it dirty white?), AND a T-shirt. Hardly any wonder he had a fit.

After the incident was all over, and Harry had regained consciousness, the Head telephoned the boy's parents to inform them of his blackout, and persuade them to get him checked by his GP. The Boss refused to acknowledge that this was an epileptic fit, and told me that as I wasn't a qualified doctor I had no right putting these ideas into people's minds. I argued that all of the classic symptoms were there even including the burning smell that comes from the mouth, but the Boss insisted and only told his parents that their son had passed out, possibly due to the heat, and needed to see a doctor. I was too inexperienced and unsure of myself to argue my case, so conceded.

In hindsight, I regret being so weak, and I only hope that Harry hasn't taken another fit at the wheel of a car and killed himself or some innocent third party because of my lack of assertiveness.

It wouldn't happen now - but then age and experience are great confidence builders.

These two incidents alone would have been enough to deter any teacher, but as they say things come in three's and in my case this was true. Also the old adage of saving the best (or was it worst) till last, comes to mind.

It was now summer, so no surprise that the weather outside was terrible. I had decided to take my class for indoor cricket. One of the teams was getting well beaten by the other, so, the losing team cajoled 'Sir' to join them

Needing VERY little prompting, I joined the losing side.

Taking middle and off guard I faced their bowler. I had already seen all of the deliveries by this lad during the lesson, so I knew exactly how to play him. As the ball thundered towards me I opened my shoulders for the inevitable boundary, swung the willow towards it and . . .

. . . C-R-A-C-K . . .

I was left with only the bat handle in my grasp. The blade of the bat was flying, like a guided missile, towards the face of one of my boxing team.

Poor Nicky took it full in the face, and all I could do was stand and watch.

Everything happened in slow motion, just like in one of the old "Kung Fu" episodes on

TV. The blade seemed to take an eternity before it struck and Nicky's head snapped back. Then his body went crashing to the ground.

Incredibly, before it touched down, he was in my arms.

To this day I have no recollection of reacting. All I remember is just standing, mouth wide open, staring in disbelief, but there he was definitely in the crook of my left arm, with three fingers of my right hand plugging the hole where his nose used to be.

I dragged him towards the Headmaster's office, where the School's only first aid kit was sited. The Boss insisted on this so that he could keep a check on all accidents that occurred in HIS school, - BUT he wasn't prepared for this one!

He shot out of his chair like a scalded cat; hair stood on end and screeching "Call an ambulance. Get a first aider. Lay him down, No stand him up. Put him in a recovery position" as he erratically orbited the room like a misguided satellite.

"Already done, Boss." I replied calmly "Ambulance is on its way."

I sounded as if I was in total control but inside I was in almost as much turmoil as he was. – Well, actually, ALMOST

- but fortunately, NOT QUITE.

When all was taken care of, and after the ambulance had left, the feeling hit me. I didn't know if I was going to faint or vomit - probably both.

I had to ask the Head to get another member of staff to cover my next lesson and I just sat outside on the school steps, head in my hands, thinking about Poor Nicky and reflecting on the mistake I had made going into the teaching profession.

*   *   *   *   *   *

If these three events were the only extraordinary incidents in my time at Harry Mac's that would have been enough. They were certainly the worst, but being the School it was, meant that there was always something happening. It certainly kept a young 'green' teacher on his toes.

Like the first time I took the fifth year to Tilery Sports Centre. I didn't know exactly what the kids could do there, so I relied on the permanent staff.

For one young troublemaker this wasn't enough.

"Reg," I asked, "this young feller said that they normally have boxing when they come here?"

"Not this week," he said, "No coach. He rang in sick this morning. They can choose from badminton, basketball, 5-a-side, table tennis or roller skating."

"There you are son, you heard the options. What's your choice?"

The lad wasn't happy and snapped "Table

Tennis, but there'd better be boxing next week"

I was fuming and yelled, "Get yourself upstairs to table tennis and less of your lip."

The lad climbed the spiral staircase, still chuntering but fortunately for him inaudible this time. If he had said one more word I would have made him take his sports shoe off and whacked him across the backside with it. Fortunately corporal punishment was allowed in those days – I rarely used it, but it was a great deterrent.

I went outside to check on the roller skaters, then back inside the main building to check out the basketballers, etc., in the sportshall. I'd only been in there about 5 minutes when the swing doors burst open and 'angry young man' entered, picked up a badminton racquet, and forced himself into the game that had been playing happily for some time without him.

"What's his name?" I asked the closest BB player.

"Doddy Cartwright, Sir" the player replied.

"CARTWRIGHT," I bellowed, "I thought You were playing table tennis"

"It's crap" he replied tersely.

I strode over, "Well *they* were getting along nicely without your interruption."

"If you want to join in, I will sub you in after they've played a few more points."

Cartwright seemed to agree and stepped to the side of the court.

I returned to the basketball game, when I heard a crash behind me.

Cartwright threw the racquet to the floor and

was striding through the doors, shouting

"This is crap I'm going back upstairs."

Then he spun to face me and said, "I'm warning you, Wuff, there'd better be boxing next week."

That was it, I'd snapped; as the red mist started to envelop my eyes I raced out of the sportshall, almost taking the doors of their hinges. I saw him halfway up the stairs.

"Cartwright, get down here. Get in the changing rooms and put your school clothes back on"

A look of apprehension flashed across his eyes. "It was only a joke, Sir"

"I didn't find it funny, Cartwright. Get your clothes on,"

I turned, to see that 80% of the sportshall was now standing, watching in the foyer.

"That wasn't a sign for you lot to stop working. Get back to your activities."

I bounded up the stairs to check on the table tennis and then leapt back down again to see that all was well in the sportshall. When I was assured, I snook out to go see Cartwright in the changing rooms. He was just pulling his jumper over his school shirt as I grabbed him by the collar.

"Ever talk to me like that again" I yelled as I pushed him up against the wall, "and I will flatten you"

Then I pulled him away from that wall and bounced him onto the adjacent one. The look of apprehension had turned to outright fear.

"Now finish getting changed, and write me an essay on the correct way to behave in my lessons"

"But Sir . . ."

"No buts, and no more protests Cartwright" I said, pushing him back to the original wall, "I'll take the essay at break tomorrow"

"But Sir . . ."

I tightened my grip on him,

"I said no more buts, Cartwright. Just **be** there tomorrow, or this will be nothing compared to what you'll get."

I turned to walk out, but had an enormous crowd to contend with. The whole of the Sportshall was there again.

"I thought I'd told you lot . . ."

I didn't finish the sentence. They all scattered. The sportshall was once again replenished.

Next morning, I recounted the story to my head of PE, Willy Hoggart

"You did what? Well, I'll tell you now, you won't get an essay off him, cos he can't read or write. And, as soon as Mr. Cartwright finds out about it he'll be over here to bounce you off the changing room walls."

"No wait a minute! You might be alright, Mr.Cartwright is in Durham Jail, and I think his eldest son, Hoss, is in with him. Mind you, it was only a few weeks ago that Mrs. Cartwright pulled a carving knife on the Boss and chased him across the quadrangle for caning her son. So you're not safe yet !"

Still feeling a bit uneasy at this revelation, I went to answer a knock on the staffroom door. There, towering above me was the skinny, six foot frame of Doddy. It was obvious how he got his nickname; his shock of unkempt, dark hair and protruding teeth made him almost the double of Ken Dodd.

"Sir, I'm really sorry, I didn't mean anything . . . but I couldn't do the essay cos I can't write." The pathetic expression on his face almost had ME convinced of his genuity.

" I understand that, Cartwright, but that sort of behaviour can't go unpunished. Step next door into the gym, and take your trainer off."

Obediently, he enter the gym/assembly hall, and I slippered him – just once, but hard. He walked out without saying a word.

I spent the rest of the week on Mrs Cartwright alert. Every time someone dashed past I had this vision of Norman Bates, from Psycho, bearing down on me, carving knife held aloft . . . but nothing happened.

Me & Doddy became best mates. In fact in a P.E. lesson a few weeks later he explained how he always fancied himself as a boxer, and would it be possible to start a boxing club in the school?

Inspired by him, I did this. We became quite good and later in the year I entered several boys for the Yorkshire Schoolboys championships. Doddy wasn't one of them, but one of the first years, a little Indian boy called Ranjit, became Champion. I later became Cleveland Schools

Boxing Secretary.

Doddy stuck at the boxing, and really enjoyed it. Every week he trained hard, and came up to me (wanting to get his own back) and said. "D'yu fancy a spar with me, Sir, before we finish ?"

Every week I obliged. Every week I said "Keep your guard up, Doddy, or you'll get one in the face."

Every week Doddy didn't keep his guard up and left with blood trickling out of his nose saying "That was great, Sir, same again next week?"

I never got any more trouble from Doddy. Unfortunately, the rest of the staff did.

The Boss also had to contend with Mrs Cartwright once more after he caned him for bullying. But, not me; Doddy was my big mate.

The last time I saw Doddy, I was waiting for a bus on Stockton High Street when the sky suddenly turned black. I looked up to see where the sun had gone and noticed an enormous figure was blocking it out. He was six foot four, enormous shoulders enhanced by a gangster style jacket with padded shoulders, and an even bigger, more unruly, shock of dark hair than I previously remembered.

"Mr. Masters isn't it ?" Doddy said.

"Yes," I said squeakily, fearing that he'd come for retribution.

"Can I buy you a pint. You know you and Mr. Bailey were the best teachers in the School."

"I'd love to, Doddy," I said truthfully, "but I'm on my way to a rugby match and I think I'm already gonna be late. But, next time we bump into each other – that's a definite"

And do you know, I meant it.

I'd never turn a drink down anyway, but, unfortunately, I never saw Doddy again.

D'you know, after writing this, I might just look him up!

I recounted this tale to Paddy Bailey next time I saw him ('cos in the meantime we'd both moved on to other schools) and he laughed.

"I only became Doddy's hero," Paddy said, "because he came to me one week before leaving school and asked me if I would teach him to read. He'd landed a job working for the Council as a gardener, and he wanted to be able to read the seed packets. So I took him for half an hour every lunchtime and showed him the pictures on seed packets and he wrote out and memorised their names. There was no way in five days that I was going to teach him to read properly," Paddy chuckled, "but Doddy was delighted."

Do you know, Harry's was a rough old School. I hated the majority of my time there, but there were some happy moments and *some* good kids. Doddy wasn't one of them, but I'll never forget him.

I can't remember any of the classes that I'd describe as a "good class" but I can remember the bad ones:- 4b stands out in particular as they needed to be kept on a tight rein all of the time. I particularly remember a cricket lesson when, as happened too often, it was heaving it down outside. So I quickly declared it an indoor bowling lesson as the class changed.

I went off to the staffroom to 'borrow' a newspaper.

The idea was to teach the kids bowling style with tennis balls, and then to put a sheet of newspaper on the gym floor 20 yards away (the room was *just* big enough) and test them for accuracy.

Twenty eight tennis balls were given out, and at the end of the lesson the class were told " Put your tennis balls in the basket on your way into the changing rooms. Get a good shower"

As they were changing I counted the balls - TWENTY SEVEN.

I looked around the hall. Nowhere to be seen. So I stormed into the changing room,

"SIT DOWN & SHUT UP. Twenty Eight tennis balls were given out and only twenty seven were returned. Who's got it?"

As expected, nobody owned up, so I said.

"Right then, the bell is going to go in three minutes, but nobody will go home until the missing ball turns up. I'm going to go to the staffroom for a cup of coffee, and when I return I expect the ball to be in the middle of the floor. *Then* you can go home, no questions asked. BUT if the ball is not there you will all stay for a detention! Right then, I'll be back in three minutes."

The staffroom was just the other side of

the changing rooms, anyone leaving had to come past me, so I made the coffee with the door open. It was delicious, I took a few sips before deciding they'd had long enough, so, I walked, cup in hand, back through the gym to confront them once again.

As I opened the door, a little wimp sniffled, "It wasn't me, Sir. But I wasn't going to go with the rest of them."

The window behind him was open – No tennis ball – No class.

Next lesson with 4b, I took the register with a size eleven plimsoll in my hand.

"Adams" – WHACK !

"Anderson" – WHACK, and so on until every one of the escapees had been punished.

Of course, some of the brighter lads knew what was coming and didn't turn up. So I declared. "Tell Jamieson, Lambert, Nicholson and Wright that if I have to come and find them I will slipper them three times, once for this one that they've missed, once for skiving off my lesson, and once for making me come to get them. . . I'll give them 'til break tomorrow, *then* I'm coming looking !"

Of course the four absentees came to see *me* and took their punishment without question.

Without doubt, Harry Macs was not my most favourite school that I'd worked in, so as the end of the school year drew close, I once again resurrected my plans to join the RAF as a PT Officer. I'd been to the Recruitment Office on the Saturday, had a chat with the officer there about my prospects, and I'd taken the forms home to fill in at my leisure.

Now, somebody must have been looking down, laughing at me, because no sooner had I finished my draft and was ready to ink in and send, when fate stepped in.

I was teaching a class on the council fields when a figure, well known to me, came striding across the cricket outfield. It was, John Hobson, Chairman of the Rugby Club that I played for.

"I hear your School is shutting down next year.

"Yeah"

"What's your plans"

I told him about my visit to the RAF recruitment office.

"So you don't fancy staying in teaching then?" he asked.

"Nope"

"Not even if a great job came up?"

"You mean at your School?" I replied.

John was Head of PE in the best rugby school in the Town, probably the County.

"Well, it would be the only job that would keep me in teaching!" I exclaimed

"The interviews are next month, so put your application in. I will be recommending you. I don't think they will go against my judgement." With that he shook my hand, turned and was gone.

I couldn't believe what had just happened. Everybody wanted that job. Maybe I could delay my RAF application just a month to see what happens.

*   *   *   *   *   *

Several schools were being closed down or amalgamated in Cleveland County that year, so teachers, who suddenly found themselves school-less, were asked to fill in an application form, putting in rank order the jobs they were interested in.

I only put down the one job – Parkside School.

The panel questioned me about this anomaly, but I stuck to my guns – Parkside or the RAF.

And so I remained a teacher for another two years.

Chapter 2

Parkside

Parkside was an old traditional grammar school. Huge playing fields skirted the long drive that divided them from the Victorian school buildings. Girls school at the start of the drive, and boys school at the far end. An asphalt running track was sited in the top left hand corner of these enormous fields, and numerous tennis courts lined the top side of the drive.

Prior to all schools going 'Comprehensive' the tennis courts were the furthest extent that the girls were allowed to go up the grounds. On no account were they allowed to fraternise with the boys. In fact, their uniform included a sash around the middle which had a whistle attached that they were to blow if any boys came too close !

Of course, the boys and girls wanted to get close; much to the annoyance of the Headmistress who once stood up in assembly to complain about a report that girls had been seen having intercourse with boys through the tennis courts netting. To this day I don't think she knows why the whole assembly fell about in hysterical laughter.

This place was a dream compared to my last school

Nothing could have contrasted more with Harry Mac's.

The staff were more strait laced and academic; sadly mostly out of touch with the real world – but they were in for a rude awakening. The upper four years in the school were grammar school intake but the first year was comprehensive. Many of these kids coming from the nearby 'working class' estate.

They struggled to read and write never mind study French, Algebra, and Chemistry.

There were two attempts in my first year there to burn the school down, as, like many of the staff, the new kids couldn't cope either.

The first attempt failed miserably because the would-be arsonists simply pushed lighted paper through the letterbox. It did manage to burn a small hole in the doormat, but as the entrance area was all stone pillars and marble, there was nothing else flammable to advance the flames. This was the level of intelligence the old grammar school staff were struggling to deal with. Not so me, after Harry Mac's any school was a doddle.

Learning from their first mistake, the fledgling arsonists made a better go of it next time. Approximately 3 weeks after the first attempt, the kids broke into the staffroom and set fire to a load of books that were sitting on foam & vinyl chairs.

Their intention of having the school closed was still thwarted by the construction of the building, The stonework stopped the flames from spreading, but the putrid fumes that came from the chairs caused another 8 classrooms to be closed due to smoke damage.

The perpetrators were caught quite easily by the police. Two eleven year old lads from the local estate who just couldn't resist bragging about what they'd done.

The staff were shell-shocked; they'd never experienced anything like this before. As for me, no problem at all. It was all in a day's work.

In fact I found the kids from the estate often easier to work with than the grammar school lot. They were generally less devious. The clever kids would try it on all the time, but knew just when to stop. Only occasionally would they over step the mark and be punished.

A typical example of this was a lesson I was covering for an absent colleague. It was a Design lesson, or CDT as the kids knew it. I wasn't too happy at giving up my free period, so was already in a bad mood; even more so as it was a bitter cold winter's day and the lesson was outside the lovely warm main building, in the Nissan huts. Fortunately the caretaker had put some extra portable heaters into the class, so after braving the icy, piercing wind, I wasn't too distressed. The class weren't too happy to see me either as I had already built up a reputation as a disciplinarian. So, when I said they had work to do, they knew I meant it – all except Wilkinson that is!

There's always one who tries to show the rest how far he can push the teacher.

I was determined to keep my reputation intact.

After the second time that I'd warned him about lounging back in his chair and not working, I threatened that he would get extra homework if he stopped once more.

That did the trick, he got his head down and I didn't have to speak to him again. UNTIL, I realised I'd left some books I needed back in the PE staffroom. So, I warned the class "I'm going to have to pop out for a minute to get some books I need. That's not a sign for you lot to stop working – *especially you Wilkinson !*"

Then I dashed outside and braved the elements again.

I knew instinctively that as soon as the class saw my back disappear across the quadrangle that they would stop working and post a lookout for me coming back. However, being just as devious as they were, I didn't return the way I left, I went through the school's corridors, past them, and emerged from a door further down the drive - behind them. Sure enough, one boy was keeping guard, the class were having a riot, and Wilkinson was leaning against the back window; his feet up on the desk, and an enormous smirk on his face.

I sneaked up behind him, and rapped sharply on the window to panic him.

It worked he did panic! The whole window disintegrated and fell in around him!

Wilkinson jumped up to attention, mouth open, eyes like saucers.

I gulped, tried to look composed, and said. "If you had been working like I told you, that wouldn't have happened Wilko !"

"Now go and find the caretaker and get a brush and shovel, AND CLEAN THIS MESS UP."

Ashen faced, Wilko left, and I said to the class "Now you lot can get back on with the work you should have been doing."

There wasn't a murmur from the class as they worked twice as hard, so as not to upset the new 'psychopath' who was teaching them.

I realised that the window glass must have shattered like that as the freezing outdoor temperature allied with the super warm indoor one must have left it particularly brittle, so the slightest tap and . . . well, you know the rest.

It was now my turn to rock back in my chair as my nerves started to calm a little. Reputation not just intact but enhanced, I tried to act nonchalant, as if this sort of thing happened every day. Inside, though my mind was racing:- *what would be the repercussions of this?*

Simple – *none* - - - except that no pupil pushed his luck with me for at least another month!

*   *   *   *   *

The next incident I experienced also involved The quadrangle outside the CDT hut, but this time, it came from the P.E. side.

Billy Jenkinson had been carried off from a rugby game with a badly swollen lower leg. I thought it was probably broken, so I phoned for an ambulance. The paramedics took hardly any time to arrive; as the ambulance station was less than 2 miles away. Before I knew it they were on a mobile phone to me from the school entrance, asking for exact directions to the injured boy. I told them to come the full length of the drive to the quadrangle and I would meet them there.

So, I asked Billy to put one arm around my shoulders and I supported him as he hopped through the changing rooms to the entrance door. It was slow progress, and by the time we got there one of the paramedics was waiting.

"Mr. Masters? I'll give you a hand with him, my mate is just reversing the ambulance to the door"

"OK, thanks," and we hobbled outside, with Billy, into the quadrangle.

"Right, Charlie, keep coming," shouted the ambulance man.

"Right, that'll do stop there," - *but Charlie didn't stop.*

"Stop !" - *but Charlie just kept coming*

S-T-O-P !!! yelled his mate but Charlie just kept coming - only slowly - but he obviously still didn't see or hear us.

Simultaneously, we both wriggled free of Billy's grip to bang on the sides of the ambulance.

Fortunately, this time Charlie heard, but, not before he had made contact with the injured boy. Billy, had, in self defence, put both hands out in front and as the ambulance contacted, he had slowly toppled over like a big pine tree.

When we raced back around the van, only his head and shoulders were visible from beneath the ambulance.

Charlie, had also run around to the back to make sure there was no more injuries on top of the broken leg. Then, fearing being reported, started jabbering about how he couldn't see us through his wing mirrors and didn't know that we'd come out the changing rooms, etc.

I comforted him and said all's well that ends well, no harm done, anyone can make a mistake, and numerous other clichés that I thought helped. Throughout this Billy said nothing, he just stared wide-eyed in a state of shock, obviously reflecting on the fact that it was safer to play rugby than go to hospital in Stockton.

*   *   *   *   *

Whilst I was at my second school I continued as County Schools Boxing Secretary, so, of course, ran a boxing club in the school.

A very successful boxing club. At the end of its first year we had produced four Yorkshire Champions.

One of the boys, Nigel Goddard, a third

year, made the England finals, and was rewarded with extra training sessions until the big day.

It was during one of these sessions that the School's renowned and well disliked wind up merchant, Jimmy Marples, decided to have a pop. Marples was the talk of the staffroom. I can't think of one teacher that had a good word to say for him – except for the P.E. staff that is. He was one of the star players in the fifth year rugby team so generally regarded the sports teachers as undeserving targets. But this day, he had the devil in him and decided to have a go.

I was sparring with Nigel in the school gym, and, to be fair, was taking a few punches on the nose. The lad was good, he had really fast hands and a lot of the time I just couldn't spot his counter-punches coming. He was a certainty for the National title.

Just as my head snapped back for the umpteenth time, Marples had finished his rugby session and was banging the mud off his boots on the wall just below the gym window.

"Hey, Parko, come and look at this, Masters is getting a good hiding from one of the third years." Marples shouted; loud enough for his comments to be heard through the single-glazed gym window.

His second row ally from the School rugby team, Anth Parkinson, came to gloat.

"If I was in there I'd knock his bleedin' head off. – But he can only box the little kids!"

That was it, I'd had enough – pummelled from one side by Nigel and insulted on the other by the School loudmouth, I said to Nige "Take minute, son"

I strode angrily out of the gym just as Marples stepped into the changing rooms. A heavily padded boxing glove hit him forcefully in the sternum and took him off his feet. As he lay on the floor with his mouth agape, I towered over him and said "I've had enough of you Marples. Tell your father I want to see him tomorrow"

Of course, Mr. Marples didn't contact, and I pretended to forget about the incident – until the next time! But, unsurprisingly, there wasn't a next time. Jimmy Marples didn't upset me ever again.

As for Nige, he continued his hard training and went to the England finals held at Pontin's Holiday Camp, Southport. His father and myself had a very enjoyable boozy weekend there, but for Nigel it was careful diet and early to bed. Next day at the weigh in, we saw his opponent for the first time. He looked nowhere near as lean and well toned as Nigel. So, we were not surprised that he failed to make the weight.

"What happens now ? Nigel asked.

"Well, if it's a close thing the lad will try to make the weight and they'll offer to weigh him again in an hour's time. But if he fails that one, he's out, and you win by default"

"So what's he gonna do?"

"Well my guess is he'll put on all the sweatshirts & tracksuits he's got and go out for a jog to try sweat the weight off."

Sure enough, about five minutes later Nigel's oppo came jogging past us, dressed up to the eyeballs in ALL of his sports clothing but as well – and I'd never seen this before – *his mother's fur coat*.

I suppose, if it works . . . and it did. That evening the two boys came toe to toe in the ring. The opponent, from Liverpool, was like greased lightning. Not just his punches but his footwork too. Nigel was fast but this lad was F-A-S-T. Poor Nigel had never encountered anything like him before and his lack of experience showed. He just folded in the third round, and nothing that we told him to do worked against the Scouser.

It was only after the bout had finished that somebody told me that the lad hadn't been beaten for nearly three years and was the defending National Champion. So I suppose it was no disgrace for Nigel to be a beaten semi-finalist to this superstar.

*   *   *   *   *

In the many years that I ran boxing clubs, both in and out of school, I always upheld a high importance on self control. Boxing teaches participants self control and self confidence. I would automatically throw members out of my squad if I found them fighting outside of the ring. Only one boy was ever kicked out for bullying.

However, whilst I was at Parkside, an incident occurred that I hadn't experienced before or since. One of my Champion boxers, suddenly stopped coming to training. When I questioned him about it he seemed quite edgy, but insisted that he couldn't come to training after school because his Mum wanted him home early. I asked him why, but he didn't like to say. Anticipating that it was something personal and private, I dropped it, and told him that he was welcome back any time if the circumstances changed.

By coincidence, over coffee in the staffroom, I was talking to one of my colleagues about my boxing club and I mentioned the fact that one of my better boxers couldn't turn up because I thought he had got to go home to look after his mother. Another teacher overheard the conversation and said "I live just down the block from Mrs. Byron and there's nothing wrong with her. In fact I was talking to her in the supermarket just a few days ago and she was telling me how proud she was of John and his boxing !"

I looked aghast at this revelation. If his mother wasn't ill, or demanding that he was home early to do some chores, and he wasn't grounded; then what was behind his reluctance?

Only one thing for it, on my way back to the P.E. area I stopped by the School office and asked one of the secretaries to look up a phone number for me. By the time I had walked back to my office, the phone was ringing.

"James, it's Jean, I've got that phone number you requested, have you got a pen?"

I wrote John Byron's home phone number down then went out to take 2b for a gymnastics lesson.

When the lesson finished, I picked up the telephone and dialled the number I had been given.

"Hello Mrs. Byron, it's Mr.Masters from Parkside. Don't worry there's not been an accident and John's not in trouble, I just wanted a little chat. I know how proud you are of John and his boxing . . ." Then I went on to explain that her son hadn't been turning up for training and the excuse that he'd given. She was stunned,

So I went on, "Please, don't say anything to him, he's not in trouble, but I have him last lesson and I want to get to the bottom of this."

At the end of the lesson, I called John Byron into my office and confronted him. He broke down and started crying like a baby.

"OK, John," I said, you're not in any kind of trouble, if you just don't want to box I understand, but you always seemed to be very keen . . ."

"I am keen, Sir," he blubbered, "It's just . . . it's just." He found it difficult to get out, but eventually blurted "It's just that some lad's from

St.Bart's are waiting for me and bullying me on the way home."

Saint Bartholomew's school was next door to Parkside and shared the same campus. There was always a big rivalry between the two schools. Occasionally, violence erupted. The two headmasters and staff were working hard to nip any problems in the bud and keep a lid on things. So I wasn't surprised that something had sprung up again, *but this time* it was one of *my* Yorkshire Champion boxers who couldn't cope with it.

John explained to me that shortest way for him to go home was through a cut next to St Bart's School and that four older boys were lying in wait for him there. They hadn't actually hurt him greatly – yet – but on two occasions that he had walked past them, they had jostled him, roughed him up a little and told him that he thought he was big being a 'Yorkshire Champion', so that the next time he comes through 'their' cut they were going to give him a boxing lesson !

So, John said, he hadn't walked that way for weeks. He took the long route home, nearly two miles longer, and by the time he'd walked that slowly, his mother thought that he'd been to training.

John seemed a lot happier to get that off his chest; so I suggested a plan.

He would come to boxing that night – which he appeared delighted to do, until his expression changed to apprehension, and then I said I would walk him home through the cut. John still seemed hesitant but agreed.

He was like a young puppy at training, hitting the bags and skipping like a Dervish, chatting away with all his old friends; but then, at the end of the session, his mood changed, as it dawned on him what was about to happen.

We both walked steadily across the School's playing fields, until we came to the junction where the two schools met. In the cut, from a distance, we could see four figures. "Is that them, John?"

"Looks like them, Sir."

"Right you walk on ahead. Don't worry I'll only be ten metres behind. I just want to see how they react to you."

Hesitantly, John walked on. Sure enough when he entered the cut the yobs circled round him and started to say things I couldn't quite hear.

"FRIENDS OF YOURS, JOHN?" I shouted

The lads swung round, and the one who appeared to be the ring leader opened his mouth, "Who the f*** are you?"

"I'll tell you who I am, sonny," I spat back, "I'm his boxing coach, and if he has any more problems coming through this cut, I'm gonna give YOU," I stared straight into the ringleaders eyes, "a boxing lesson."

"There's four of us," he said.

I turned to John and said "Get home now John" then I quickly spun round on the loudmouth and said with venom "Listen, sunshine, there might be four of you but if you start up, it's YOU that I'm gonna put in hospital. The rest of your mates might give me a good hiding but I've memorised all of your faces. I'll get you one at a time even if it takes me years. AND, I'm sure that Mr. Sheraton, will give me a hand to find out where you all live."

John Sheraton, was head of PE at St. Bart's, and the mention of his name put a different complexion on things for these scumbags.

"You teachers are all the f*****g same," Mouthy said, as he stepped aside.

"Just wait till I leave school"

Stepping through the gap, I walked back towards Parkside, then spun on my heels again, and said "When you leave school, sonny, you'll be a member of the public. I won't take this crap from you then. I'll knock your f*****g teeth down your throat."

The bluff seemed to work, John Byron came to the next dozen or so training sessions, and then suddenly stopped.

I didn't bother him about it again, – you can only do so much.

*   *   *   *   *

The other big change I encountered at Parkside was GIRLS. I'd not taught them before. And I didn't here either - lower down the school – but fifth year P.E. was mixed. The boys and girls (well, young adults really) chose which option they fancied; from basketball, volleyball, badminton, table tennis, etc., then picked up teams, and got on with it. The PE staff just patrolled to see that everything was running smoothly; *sometimes* they joined in.

"Fancy a game of volleyball, Sir?" one of the boys shouted across to me, "we're one short."

Welcome of a break from the monotony, I joined the team that only had five. Both teams had four males, and two females in their number and one of the females was Judy Green!

Judy was the pin up of the School, *and she knew it*. I was surprised any of the young boys got any work done in her classes because in P.E. their eyes, out on stalks, followed here every move.

She loved it, and played on it. Rather than tying her long blonde (bottle blonde) hair back like a sportswoman would, she deliberately let it hang over her shoulders so that she could flick it back and play with it, She deliberately wore the tightest P.E. clothes that she could fit into, so that her long legs, nicely rounded backside and ample boobs were accentuated, Her face wasn't anything outstanding, but I don't think any of these sixteen year old boys ever noticed that.

Judy was on my side, and was quite a good sportswoman, *when she wasn't posing*. So I was quite surprised when it came to my turn, on the rotation to serve, that she took the ball and walked to the baseline.

"My serve, Judy," I said raising my hands to receive the ball.

"No, it's my turn," she replied, "I was in the middle."

"Well now, that's where you've got it wrong, the player at the top right moves back to serve." I held my hands out again.

"That's not how we've always played it here" she argued back.

"Well, they're the proper rules, so that's how we'll play it from now on."

She held the ball out for me, and just as I grabbed it pulled it into her breasts and started to move it up and down. I dropped the ball like a hot cake and visibly flushed. The whole of the volleyball game erupted in laughter whist I, like a spoilt child, blurted out "If you're not going to play the game properly, I'm putting the ball away. You can all choose another option."

"Aw, come on Sir, it's just a laugh." They all shouted in unison.

I turned and threw the ball back. "Well, I don't see the joke! Anyway I've got to check on the other groups."

I strode away, still embarrassed, but more worried that the kids, as they do, would exaggerate this story and it would evolve into me initiating the situation.

To be fair I never heard the volleyball game mentioned again, I didn't again join that group, and Judy never came to apologise to me.

However, I didn't seek Judy out for an apology either, – or *anything else.*

*　　*　　*　　*　　*

I left Parkside at the end of my second year, not because I didn't like the School, but because of external circumstances.

I had gone through a particularly stressful marriage, in which my wife couldn't put up with the loneliness of her husband coming in late most evenings after either playing or coaching sport. I took the stance that while we were courting she was quite happy to be engaged to a teacher and sportsman, but now that we were married she wanted me tied to the kitchen sink.

She took the position that, while we were courting she lived at home with her parents and her sisters, but now she was in a house on her own she couldn't cope.

So, being the compassionate fella that I am, I packed in the Monday night boxing coaching, and Friday night League basketball and was only left with my rugby.

She still wasn't happy and said "Surely, as a PE teacher, you're fit enough and don't need the two training nights on top of the Saturday game!"

Trying desperately to save the marriage I agreed to drop the Tuesday session, but told her "It's not just about fitness training. Thursday is tactics. I need to be at that one as well as Saturday. I'm not dropping any more. - Before they go, *you go*"

Of course, eventually she went, but not before we both tried one last throw of the dice. Still moaning about my two days that I still reserved for sport, I suggested a solution to her boredom. Why didn't she come to watch my next game, when Stockton played Sandal?

She had never seen me take part in anything since we'd met, and I thought this might be a solution.

Lady Luck was smiling on her that day as the weather was glorious, which was just as well, because she totally ignored my advice that it might be best to wear jeans and trainers to the match. I left her in the car, wearing her mini-skirt and stiletto's while I went in to change. I informed her "I'll be back out in about twenty minutes, but we'll just run straight out to the pitch, so, "You follow us over. I'll be wearing the red number ten shirt."

Vanity had also stopped her bringing her glasses.

When the match finished, I asked her, "Did you enjoy that?" as I thought she might have been impressed with the try I scored.

She replied, "I was bored. You didn't do much"

"I thought I had a good game" I said, but she disagreed. However, on further questioning I discovered that she had stood between the two pitches with her back to the

First Team game that I was in. – Apparently the Third Team Fly Half didn't have much of a game – according to her.

Anyway, divorce followed, and totally fed up with life in general, I quit my post at Parkside School, sold my house, sold my car, and took up the offer of a friend of mine to play rugby in the USA.

Chapter 3

I Quit

My plane touched down in Toronto, I could have flown to New York but it was much more expensive than Canada and just about the same distance away from my final destination of Ann Arbor; Michigan.

I was glad I chose this option because the airline I flew with, the Canadian Company Wardair, were superb. The 5 hour flight passed by in no time at all, probably a lot due to the free drinks they served up throughout the trip, (I had five double whiskies) but also because the in-flight meal was excellent. How many times can you say that about airline food ? – But the mini–steak, mushrooms & chips that they served would not have been out of place in any restaurant.

It was probably memorable, moreso, because this was also my first flight ever; I'd been abroad several times before, but always to Europe and always by either coach, or train. So much of my delight at this experience was probably down to the novelty of it all. Nevertheless, on reflection however, even as a very well travelled oldie now, I would still be delighted to travel with the same Company.

The flight touched down in the early hours of the morning, and as I staggered down the plane's steps I wished I'd put my jacket on, as the August night wind carried an icy bite. My plan had been to sleep on the plane and then either stay in the airport terminal, or wander around downtown Toronto until my greyhound bus left at 11 am. But as they say; all the best plans . . . I was too tired (drunk) to do that so I hailed a cab (already speaking American) and naively asked the driver to take me to the nearest decent hotel that was open. Of course he took me, undoubtedly, to the hotel that gave him the best commission.

The Holiday Inn *was* superb, but it cost me two weeks wages for just a few hours sleep. I'd have been happy with a Salvation Army hostel.

If this doesn't illustrate the evils of drink, what else does?

Anyway, I had a great night's sleep, then showered and dressed into my best casuals before setting out for the bus station. All my worldly goods were packed into a rucksack so I walked there – mainly to compensate for the previous night's overspend but also to clear my head, and because I needed to economise, as I wasn't sure exactly how much it was going to cost me to spend a month in America.

I had only walked a few blocks when one of the natives grabbed my arm and roughly jerked me back onto the 'sidewalk' as a huge car almost ran over my toes.

"You're English aren't you?" my new found friend asked.

I nodded.

"Well don't forget we drive on the right over here, buddy."

I thanked him, and he left.

Lesson number one learned!

*   *   *   *   *

I had arranged to meet up with Brad, my host and club vice captain at the bus station in London (Ontario). The journey there was uneventful, but then the fun started. The Club captain and another of the players accompanied Brad in his car and typical of rugby players, after the formalities of intro's and handshakes, a can of beer was thrust into my hand. So as we travelled down the freeway towards the border, I jerked at the ringpull. The hiss alerted my fellow travellers who simultaneously freaked out.

"What are you doing," Brad shouted, "it's illegal for anyone to have a can of beer open in the car. If you're going to drink, keep your head down below window level"

Lesson number two.

We may speak the same language (almost) but the cultural differences between ourselves and our closest cousins over the pond are immense.

Next experience on my learning curve was at the border!

I have been through scores of customs posts all over the world but I've never had such a going over as that day on the border between Canada & USA. The American customs official was straight out of Stalag 17. No courteousness, he just spat out questions & commands;

"What is the purpose of your visit to the United States?"

"He's coming to play for Michigan Rugby Club." Brad said.

Adolf went blue in the face and yelled at Brad, "Don't coach him. I want to hear it from HIM"

I'm here to play for Michigan Rugby Club." I said mimicking Brad.

"Where are your bags?"

I humped my rucksack onto the counter without saying a word.

"Is that it?"

"Yes"

Then he started to dismantle all of my carefully packed belongings onto the work top. Fortunately the rucksack had no lining or padding, otherwise I think he would have ripped that apart too. I looked at his fellow officer who was standing by silently. I whispered "Did he get out of the wrong side of the bed, or is he always like this?"

His colleague said nothing, but just raised his eyebrows and smirked. Enough said.

"Shut up!" Adolf roared, "Are you carrying any drugs about your person?"

"Never use them, mate." I said – which was the truth.

Adolf didn't like being called mate. He was nobody's 'mate.'

I gulped, regretting winding him up. I could sense a strip search coming on.

"You won't mind us patting you down, then. Empty your pockets onto the bench".

I was relieved. I decided there and then not to wind Adolf up anymore – he didn't need it – he was already wound up to maximum..

"OK you're free to go. Have a nice journey." Herr grupen fuehrer said with little feeling.

"It's been wonderful up to now." I said. (couldn't resist). Then I almost sprinted through the exit door just in case he pulled me back to have another go.

Outside, I took a deep breath of American air as I stood in the USA for the first time.

*   *   *   *   *

I had plenty of escapades while I was in the US, but, trying to stick as closely as I can to this book's remit, they'll be left until the next one.

I had arranged to stay with Brad and his wife, DeeDee, for one month, but part way through, decided it was time to go touring after our excessive drinking almost caused a divorce. Brad wasn't normally much of a drinker but had been pushing the boat out while I was there. This was causing some friction, but everything erupted after the night when we both staggered in a bit more intoxicated than usual. Part way through this night, Brad had a nightmare and during it, punched Dee Dee in the mouth. Then rolled over and went soundly back to sleep despite her sobbing and nagging.

At breakfast Brad was really apologetic, but Dee Dee was having none of it; she just sat there fuming; one lip three times bigger than the other.

I said nothing, but was secretly planning my escape. Now was a good time to cash in my Ameripass ticket.

The Ameripass ticket, (*highly recommended*) – gave me 15 days unlimited travel on Greyhound buses You can purchase them for longer - but they have to be purchased in advance *abroad* – ie. Only for tourists.

So, I set off on my great adventure to California. *(Beach Boys inspired, - and what an adventure!)*

I had worked out that I could only afford to sleep in a cheap hotel every third night, so two had to be spent on the bus *(not recommended!)*. I purchased an inflatable pillow that I had noticed were easily available through vending machines, at the Bus Stations.

Fortunately, most buses weren't full so I had a double seat to myself most of the time. I simply jammed the pillow against the window and within minutes, the drumming of the wheels on the freeway sent me to sleep. It wasn't the most comfortable night's sleep I'd ever had but it served its purpose. Courtesy stops were frequent, and most of the 'restrooms' at these stations had shower facilities, so I happily covered thousands of miles like this, taking in Chicago, St. Louis, Kansas City, Tulsa, Dallas, El Paso, Los Angeles, San Francisco, Salt Lake City, Omaha, and finally New York; before returning to Ann Arbor. Prior to going out to the States my dream had been to visit LA and of course Hollywood - the original Disney World and Universal Studios in Annaheim. So I allocated three days there.

I wasn't disappointed!

When I returned to Brad's I had only one more game to play for Michigan before I flew home. My money was almost gone, and none of the leads I had put out bore fruit, employment-wise. It seemed that Ann Arbor, being a university town, was the wrong place to get work in. All the casual jobs were taken by the students, and all the low paid jobs by the blacks. (I'm not a racist, in fact quite the opposite, but that was just the way it was)

So, - disappointed and penniless, - I returned to Britain.

My mother was pleased to see me, and I was able to live with my parents rent free until I found a job.

I went to the JobCentre - *(very depressing)* - and was asked, what qualifications I had.

"Qualified teacher" I replied.

"Then you're qualified for NOTHING; except teaching" the cheerless assistant told me. (I think Adolf's sister must have emigrated to England.)

"What sort of job do you want ?"

"Absolutely anything," I replied, "I can turn my hand to anything"

She thrust a card into my hand. "This company needs a sales rep., do you think you could do that?"

"No problem." I responded.

As a student I'd had numerous holiday jobs; as a dustman, twice in laundries, twice with British Steel – cleaning out the rolling mills and working in the chemical laboratories and in numerous pubs as a barman. So I was confident that I could take on anything.

"I'll give them a ring and arrange an interview" Adolfette informed.

On the following Friday I was being interviewed by the manager. It turned out that the job that I was looking forward to as 'sales rep' with a flashy company car was as a carpet salesman in a shop with the occasional use of a van for deliveries.

Still, beggars can't be choosers.

The interview went great until I told him I was an ex-teacher.

Then his face changed and he told me it was company policy not to employ ex-teachers or policemen, as they are too bossy, – but that he was going to make an exception in my case. So I was offered the job.

Great ! now I can get down to saving for my return to Michigan again. But when he told me the wage, it was barely enough to live on never mind open a deposit account. Still, some money is better than none. I asked him what the hours were, but then he dropped the bombshell. He said we worked Saturdays! That was the final straw. I wasn't going to give up my rugby career for a pittance – especially after being lured in by false promises.

"We've all got to make sacrifices" he explained "I'm president of Hartlepool Rovers - but I can't always make every game due to commitments."

I agreed, - everyone has to make sacrifices. – So, I sacrificed this poorly paid, deliberately misleading job as a 'sales rep'.

Still desperate for money, though, I took on another poorly paid job, as a taxi driver. The pay wasn't great, but it was nothing at all when you didn't have a fare. After the boss had taken his portion out of the fares, I was frequently left without enough to live on. I was never going to save at this rate.

So, yet again, I switched. I was taken on by a local car company, picking up brand new cars and vans from their import points, mainly in the London area, and driving them up North to local dealerships. This was a better paid job but very hit and miss as to the days I worked. I needed something more reliable.

Eureka! The idea hit me.

Why not use my other great passion, MUSIC, to prop up this inconsistent income. So, I invested some money at the local RSC store in Middlesbrough, and very soon became the proud proprietor of the 'Time of Your Life' mobile disco.

Fantastic move - I loved it!

I have a multitude of stories to tell about my DJ adventures - they would probably fill a whole book on their own (and in future probably *will*) - but suffice to say that I started in a small way – as most businesses do. I played mainly youth clubs, schools & colleges, with the occasional 21st party or wedding reception thrown in. Then, as my disco became more popular I took on some 'residencies'.

Unfortunately, though, while my disco was still in its infancy, I was putting out more money on records and equipment than I was taking in (and obviously that wasn't the idea).

So, *in desperation*, I went back to teaching.

Well – not REAL teaching; - but supply teaching.

Supply teaching was totally different to being a permanent contracted teacher because the money was better. It wasn't higher paid, it was just that you received your weeks wages with your holiday pay included, so it felt better. But the main difference, as a supply teacher was that you didn't have to prepare lessons, take books home for marking, write reports & assessments, attend parents evenings, etc.

In fact money for old rope really – if you could control kids – and as you have already found out, I had little trouble in that department.

So, I went on the 'Register', but appointments were few and far between. There wasn't much demand for supply P.E. teachers as they tended to be the healthiest on the school staff. However, fortunately for me, one day the Education Committee rang up enquiring for a school in Eston that were desperate for a Geography teacher. "Had I any experience?"

"Well, yes. I have 'O' level geography so theoretically I can teach up to that level, but I also taught it for a year in my first school."

"Great!" the secretary said, "I'll get the headmaster to contact you this afternoon. You start tomorrow, for the rest of the week."

"By the way, what other subjects do you teach?"

"Well, my second subject is Art, but I also taught metal work for a year at Parkside."

"OK, good, I'm sure we can get you loads more work."

The following day I was taking five lessons of Geography in Eston. My input was really mainly crowd control, as all the lessons were set by the Head of Department.

Then, after four days in Eston, I was given two weeks in Middlesbrough, teaching Science.

"Could I teach science ?

"Never done so, but I have 'O' level chemistry and I am a disciplinarian. If you get the Head of Science to set the work, etc. . ."

Accidentally, I had hit on the right formula. Most headteachers' simply wanted their classes 'minding' with no trouble or disruption. They weren't really bothered if, in that one off lesson, the kids learned very little.

So, consequently, I next experienced a week in Billingham teaching French.

Could I teach French ?

"No, but I have 'O' level French, etc . ."

In fact over the next few months I 'taught' nine different subjects. I was never once turned down by a headmaster when I used the phrase . . . "no - but I'm a disciplinarian. etc."

My style of 'supply teaching' was selling like hot cakes.

And as the cliché goes - "either a famine or a feast" – well, my disco was taking off too.

I had no time for car deliveries now. Most weeks I was working Monday to Friday, teaching, and on Friday nights and Saturday nights as a DJ. The money was rolling in.

Was I enjoying it?

The disco's – yes., but almost permanent supply teaching NO.

It was boring just supervising other peoples classes. I was reading stacks of books and newspapers. I became quite proficient at crosswords:- but *I was bored*. If the money hadn't been so good, I would have turned completely over to DJing.

Then came the midweek residencies

Was I going to turn them down, or could I keep teaching going as well ?

Teaching was an easy regular income. It would be stupid to turn it down, and what if the gigs dried up? – especially during the warm nights of the summer.

So, should I cut back on the disco's? Well, similarly, teaching could dry up – wouldn't teachers also be more healthy in the summer?

Problems – which I thought could only be sorted out by trial and error.

So I took on the residencies as well.

Residencies are great because they are normally in pubs, or nightclubs, that have their own equipment. So the DJ just turns up with his box of records and gets on with it.

No more to humping heavy speakers up 3 flights of stars 'cos the lift was broken. (as had often been the case).

That was the worst part a mobile DJ's job - setting up & taking down at the end of each night. Especially if you have work the next day but don't get home until 3 in the morning!

It was in the middle of this success as a DJ/teacher that I took on my younger brother Adam as an "apprentice."

It halved the workload (but didn't halve the money!)

Adam was 16 and very green, but, DJing broadened his outlook. Especially doing gigs like the club that booked us, but didn't tell us until we arrived, that it was a men only do!

No; not a gay event – but a stripperama! They only wanted us to play the dance music for the multitude of girls on display!

It took Adam nearly a week for his eyesight to return to normal.

Then, just as the disco's were booming, (as always happens), I was offered a semi-permanent job in a school.

I had already worked for two weeks in this 'rough' school in Billingham as a supply teacher, when, towards the end, the headmaster collared me in the staffroom.

"Hi, James, how's things ?"

That is normally the opening gambit which indicates 'things' are about to change.

"Fine, a couple of days left and then I can put my feet up."

"Great," the boss replied, with that sort of look on his face that told me that he was really here for an ulterior motive. "How do you fancy working here full time for the next two terms?"

I just looked at him with a quizzical expression

"Teaching Social Studies and Sociology"

Dave Zephyr, my sociology lecturer from College would have split his sides laughing, but this boss was deadly serious.

"No need to decide now, think about it overnight and let me know tomorrow" He threw a book into my lap. "It's all very easy stuff. Have a look at this, that's their course book."

Then he was gone.

That evening I read the book, cover to cover. The Boss was right, it was all very easy. I don't think I've ever read a complete text book in one evening before, but this was comic book stuff.

I mulled it over. Could I manage six months of teaching every week plus discos, every Monday, Friday & Saturday. The answer was 'definitely maybe.'

The weekends were no problem, but the Monday one might be arduous. It wasn't the DJing until 11 pm, but then it was the packing away, driving home from Redcar, unloading the van, then winding down before eventual sleep at around 2 am.

When the 7 am alarm sounded the next day, I had decided that I could cope, but only for six months. Hopefully, by then, I would have amassed enough dough for my next US rugby trip.

Then, (I should have expected it) Fate showed its hand once again.

I needn't have worried about my Redcar 'residency' as I only played one more gig before the pub landlord pulled the plug.

On that particular Monday, the Guisborough 'chapter' of the Hell's Angels decided to pay a call on some of their rivals who were regulars at my disco.

The motorbike gang, (mostly looking like spotty young kids riding Honda 50's) pushed past the bouncer on the door, located the table they were searching for and then waded in with bike chains, metal bars and bottles. In seconds, the floor was swimming in blood.

It took four ambulances to take the more injured victims away.

So, I'd only had to put up with two weeks of very little sleep on Monday nights since taking the 'sociology' job on.

The negative side though was that my Michigan kitty would be a little down, especially since, expecting to be there for a while, I'd invested in albums by Deep Purple, Black Sabbath, Led Zeppelin & Pink Floyd for my heavy metal regulars at "The Cutty Sark". I doubted they'd ever be played again in any future disco!

(*footnote: they weren't* – anybody want to buy some great Heavy Metal albums – *only played once ?*)

*   *   *   *   *

So, after being warned several times by my sociology lecturer at College that I was going to fail the course (which of course I didn't), I was now a Sociology teacher, taking my first Social Studies class. It wasn't all plain sailing as the headmaster had said (*conned again*) because twice a week I had an 'O' level Sociology group to take. This meant lots of preparation & marking to do; but to be honest, I actually quite enjoyed it. Mind you, the topic I was covering was "Work & Leisure" which also suited me.

Anyway, - I'll start again . . . there I was in my Social Studies class, when it dawned on me that most of the kids in this group had only chosen it 'cos it was a soft option -
Sitting around reading comic books – dead easy.

I think some of the class might have been troublesome to other teachers but this lot knew me as *the PE teacher* who had been there for two weeks already, and so didn't try it on – all except for one particularly unsavoury character, Micky Hatton.

As I was walking around the class I noticed Hatton openly and blatantly carving something into the desk top. So, I shoved a sheet of paper under his nose and said, "I don't care if you are not interested in this lesson Micky, *(I knew his name as I'd been warned in the staffroom)* just don't disturb anyone else. If you need to doodle, do it on the paper. Otherwise if I see anything else scratched into the desk top you will be given a sheet of sandpaper and a can of varnish, and a detention, to repair the damage."

Hatton said nothing, he just looked at me with disinterested eyes, and then started to draw on the paper.

I turned my back, and continued going through the important aspects of the first chapter of the comic book with the rest of the class. The next time I looked across at Micky Hatton, his head, not the pencil, was on the paper and he was sound asleep.

And so I suffered no further disturbances in my 'Sociology' lessons. In a curious way I also quite enjoyed taking this group. OK, they were a less able group but we developed quite a good rapport and routine with 50% comic book reading and 50% related discussion. The discussions often became quite lively & interesting.

The real success though was the more able Sociology group. Even though I was only one chapter ahead of them in the heavy duty text book, I prepared the lessons thoroughly and they were a delight to teach. But, the real bonus was that the class achieved outstanding success in the 'O' level exams. That felt good, and the class appreciated all my efforts too:- when it came to my last lesson, a couple of the girls, who had spent many lessons flirting with me, walked to the front of the class and gave a little speech that they had prepared, thanking me and wishing me luck in my next school. Then another girl walked to the front holding an enormous gold & red box neatly tied around with a red ribbon. I thanked the young ladies and told them that I was going to enjoy eating these chocolates with a nice glass of whisky whilst watching TV that evening. The girls were horrified when I put them down on the desk, and catcalled for me to open the box. Now, highly suspicious that the box didn't actually contain normal chocolates, I opened the lid very gingerly. Surprised that there was no explosion as I removed the top, I folded back the tissue paper to reveal what the girls, I'm sure, thought were a very trendy, but tight, light blue, nylon underpants.

The class howled, while I turned bright red and thanked them.

As I put the undergarments back in the box, more cat calls:

"Put them on, Put them on!!!"

How could I refuse?

I pulled the pants up and over the trousers I was wearing, and the class erupted into even more merriment.

I looked down to notice the logo that had been screen printed on the front was a clock tower standing bold and tall with the inscription "Big Ben" below it.

My face went even more scarlet!

As for the other class, they also did well in the CSE exams and I think they were actually thankful to be taught something rather than have every lesson disrupted by Micky Hatton. And as for Micky himself, he came to every lesson and caught up on his sleep. Until, that is, about half way through the term, when he failed to turn up.

"Where's Hatton?" I enquired, but not really bothered.

"He's banged up" shouted one of the lively lads at the back.

"Well, I can't say I didn't see that one coming," I retorted raising high the comic book. "Let's try page 43 today"

I wondered if it had already got round that 'Sir' was instrumental at getting Micky 'banged up'?

By coincidence, the previous Friday night I had been booked to do a disco at the local Youth Club that many of the kids from School went to.

I still did this gig as a favour, even though it was the poorest paid one on our rota and we had moved on to bigger things. This had been the first joint that my disco had performed at, as the bloke in charge was a friend of mine from Stockton Rugby Club.

So I stayed faithful to the commitment - and the price.

However, on this particular night though, something unusual happened,-
Micky Hatton turned up.

Now, Micky didn't normal come to these 'kiddies disco's as they weren't "Cool", but on this occasion while all of the uncool nerds from school were dancing, he simply sat on his own on one of the chairs at the perimeter of the dance floor. He sat there for quite a while not talking to anybody and not really looking at anybody.

I couldn't decide if he was on something or not.

Then one of the wimpy, nerdy, 15 year old lads walked past him, and he stuck out a leg and tripped him up.

The nerd swore.

In a flash, Micky jumped up, "What did you f******g say?" he yelled as he rained kicks and punches into the lads face & body.

Before, the youth worker and myself could get to the spot to pull him off, it was all over. Micky had done what he had come there for, and legged it.

The nerd's face was a real mess and needed hospital treatment, so an ambulance was called, AND the police.

Why is it always that these so called hard men (bullies) always pick on the wimpiest kids to enhance their reputation? Even when I was a schoolboy myself, I noticed that the bullies never picked on anyone from the School rugby team.

Anyway, when the police arrived I gave a statement and as soon as I mentioned the name Micky Hatton , the PC put his pen down, pulled his helmet back on, and said "Thanks. Micky Hatton, eh? I know where to find him."

Shortly, after this incident I assessed my own situation. The Headmaster had asked me to stay on for another year teaching sociology, but I turned it down. I told him that if he had offered me a PE job I might have considered it, but otherwise I was going back to the States to play some rugby.

However, when I took stock of my finances, I still only had enough to fly back to Michigan and play for a month or two – not the whole season as I wanted. The disco, although now making good money, took a lump out of my bank balance in setting up.

So I was in a quandary, do I take the sociology position again, which was regular money and I sorta liked it, or go back on the supply list hoping to pick up a PE job. I decided to sleep on it, but couldn't take *too* long as the summer holidays were fast approaching.

Then my friend FATE reared his head again.

"Hello, is that James ?" the voice on the phone asked.

"Yes"

"I hear that you are back in the country again. Are you interested in teaching again?"

"I am teaching again – supply at Bridgeford School in Billingham."

"Great! How do you fancy a job teaching PE at my school next year?"

"Where's that ?"

"Hawksmount School near Yarm."

"I think I'd better explain myself a bit better. My name is George Barton, you taught with my wife, Mary, at Parkside. There's a PE job going at my school. It's yours if you want it."

"Yeah, I'm interested, but please excuse my ignorance, where is Hawksmount ?

The Headmaster explained and invited me to visit on the following Monday morning.

"If you pop in, the Head of PE, Bob Latchford, will show you around and deal with any of your questions. So if that's OK, I'll see you Monday."

"Yeah, thanks for the offer." My head was spinning, this sounded great. I could work for 3 months and still have not missed too much of the rugby season to make it worthwhile playing for Michigan.

*　　　*　　　*　　　*　　　*

Monday morning took an eternity to arrive.

I caught the bus to Yarm and walked the short distance to the outskirts, to where the School was located.

I called in at Reception and one of the secretaries organised a pupil to take me down to the Sportshall where Mr. Latchford was taking a badminton lesson.

As I walked through the school hall I looked around and was very impressed with the surroundings. Very polite secretaries and escort - no graffiti anywhere to be seen - clean & tidy main hall and well kept gym. All good so far.

Then I entered the sportshall
-　　G-R-I-M!

Apparently, it was the first one built in County Durham, and you could tell. Black tarmac floor, grey walls and ceiling, slit windows at the top of the walls which let in very little natural daylight so the strip lights had to be on all the time, and COLD!

What a waste, and how dingy !

But there was nothing dismal about Bob Latchford's smile and his firm handshake. "Nice to see you," he said. "Good timing; this lesson's just about to finish and I'm free next, so we can chat over a coffee."

"Right lads that's it. Put the racquets in the basket, shuttlecocks in the tubes. Go and get a good shower,"

Then he turned back to me. "This'll only take a couple of minutes, then I'm all yours."

"No sweat. " I replied

We walked outside the sportshall, past a nicely kept garden area, to the staff changing room. Bob opened the door, pulled a drawer out of his desk and shouted "Valuables" as he placed it on the table outside. Then he turned back to me. "How do you like your coffee ?"

Strong, white, two sugars," I replied.

I liked this fella's easy going relaxed attitude already, I knew then that we were going to get on and I was going to take the job.

Little did I realise that this was all an act!!!

He never made me another cup of coffee in all the time I worked with him!!!

Chapter 4

Hawksmount

I felt a bit of a fraud taking on the job at Hawksmount, as I think they were looking at it as a long term appointment, and I only intended to teach a term and then disappear to salvage the rest of the rugby season in Ann Arbor.

Little did I know that Fate intended for me to be at this school for another sixteen years and even then, I didn't want to leave.

*   *   *   *   *

My first few weeks at Hawksmount were unimpressive. Bob was a good Head of PE and I just fell in with the way he ran things, and learned the ropes from him.

The biggest difference with this school than others that I'd been in was the kids – polite, well behaved. It wasn't a battle of 'us & them' as had been apparent at my other schools. I was really beginning to like working here.

But, one thing I couldn't get to grips with was that Bob kept going out of the PE staffroom on business, and continually left the door unlocked – sometimes even wide open!

I spent the first three months going behind him locking up his mistakes.

Until one day he took me to one side and said "Do you have the keys to our room? Cos some idiot has locked mine inside!"

"Oh, I locked up. Didn't realise yours were inside."

"You keep doing that – every time I go out, I come back and the rooms locked."

"Force of habit," I replied, If we didn't lock doors behind us at my other Schools, I would come back to an empty room. The kids would steal everything."

"Well, not here," he said quite shirtily, "Just leave the doors open."

"Well alright, but when you come back and everything's gone . . . "

"Just leave the doors open."

"OK," I said, "on your head be it."

So I did, and do you know, not a thing went missing.

Do you remember the incident at Harry Mac's where I had to count the tennis balls in and out for lessons?

Not here!

It even got to the stage where for basketball lessons I would shout to the kids "As soon as you're ready get a ball from the cupboard and go and warm up" and they did !

I was beginning to REALLY like this place.

The basketball cupboard, that I referred to was in the corridor leading to the gym, and was accessible to the public during evenings (when the School turned over to a Community College) and I even took to leaving the cupboard open then too, so that the Youth Club and Basketball Club could gain easy access to the balls. Incredibly, in sixteen years only one ball went missing!!!

Of course, like any school, we had a small number of 'problem' kids (but only a small number !) and generally these could be controlled by detentions, or the *threat* of corporal punishment.

I think it is a great pity that corporal punishment has been banished from schools and from availability to parents too! Its advantages by far outweigh its disadvantages. The 'do good brigade' who describe it as an extreme physical beating exaggerate to further their cause. The main advantage of CP is not physically *'beating'* a child – but the deterrent threat of it.

To this end, at Hawksmount, I had a specially prepared gym shoe that looked the part, and its mere presence often scared the 'wrongdoers' into behaving. It was a size eleven plimsoll with a red white and blue target painted on the sole and the words 'Hotshot' written in red down one side, and 'The Peacemaker' down the other.

It was impressive, but rarely used. The mere fact that I had a specially prepared implement to use showed that I meant business and was enough to psychologically persuade the kids into compliance.

It worked 90% of the time. If I had a class or individual playing up, I would often say nothing but just walk into the staff changing room and come out holding 'Hotshot'.

As I put it down on the table, you could hear a pin drop.

Like I said, it worked 90% of the time – but with one memorable exception.

A group of new first years came into the changing rooms and they were as high as kites with excitement. They were yelling & screaming in the high pitched voices that only belong to twelve year old boys. Bags and towels were being thrown around, and one or two 'little angels' were scragging each other. I stood on the bench so they could see and hear me more clearly, but even my Sergeant-Major's voice was not getting through. So I turned to get 'The Peacemaker'. I put the gym slipper down on the table where the 'valuables' are collected.

Nothing !

The mayhem continued unabated.

So I picked up Hotshot, waved it around a couple of times and placed it back on the table.

Nothing still.

So this time I picked it up and slammed it into the table-top really hard so that the sound reverberated around the small changing room walls.

Fifty pieces of a watch sprayed around the changing rooms like hailstones!

As I hadn't yet put the drawer out, one of the boys had simply placed his watch on the table and in my anger I failed to look before striking the wooden top.

The young lad just stood there dewy eyed, with his bottom lip quivering, as I used the side of my hand to sweep the few pieces that were left on the table, into my other hand.

"It's OK, son," I said, "my uncle is a watchmaker. I'll have it as good as new in no time."

Of course, it was way beyond repair. It cost me a quarter of my weeks wages to replace it. Mind you, the whole class was exceptionally well behaved from then on!

*　　*　　*　　*　　*

Also, like any other school we had our share of criminal activities. One year we went through a phase of things being stolen from the changing room. Despite warning the kids that ALL items of any worth must be handed into the 'valuables' drawer, some kids didn't, and the problem continued.

So we decided that direct action had to be taken. Whenever Bob or myself had a free period we would read a book or newspaper whilst hiding in the showers, where we could of course hear any unwanted guests come into the changing rooms.

During my fist stint on 'stakeout' after only about fifteen minutes I heard the distinctive creak of the entry door opening. I waited as the illegal entrant passed my hiding place and then gave him another minute so that I could catch him in the act. Then, I jumped up from my seat and ran round the corner bellowing.;"What do you think you're doing in here ?"

The lad was caught red handed.

He was standing at the urinal, his hair stood on end, and in reaction had peed down his leg, as he exclaimed "Jeez, Mr.Masters, I thought I was being gangbushed"

I nearly wet myself too – laughing - but I wasn't so joyful as to let this trespasser away with the 100 lines punishment required for ignoring the door notice "You are reminded that entry is for pupils attending P.E. ONLY"

The changing rooms can also be quite a daunting place for pupils that are a bit nervous about undressing in front of the other boys. It was for this reason that we always stressed that lads could wear swimming trunks under their shorts, and when they go into the showers. When the first years initially come into the school, as well as stressing this, we gave a short lecture on hygiene and our insistence that every boy showers after every PE lesson.

So, it came as quite a surprise when one of our newcomers, lied to me when I asked him if had been in the showers.

"Yes, Sir" he replied.

"Well you've been very quick, Nobody else is out. Show me your towel."

"It's bone dry – you haven't been in have you?"

The boy looked at his feet, and replied "No Sir"

"Well if this ever happens again I will give you a detention to come back and shower after school. This time I'm going to give you a second chance. *Get into the showers!* I'm going to come back in two minutes and I want to see you scubbing in there." I turned and walked away towards the staff room.

As promised, I returned a couple of minutes later, and as expected the boy was in the shower, *but not as expected,* the lad was standing under the jets with his towel still wrapped around himself!!!

"Oh, son!" I exclaimed in amazement, "Now what are you going to dry on?"

The lad said nothing, but just looked at me sheepishly.

"Stay there, while I go and get a clean towel."

We always had a stack of clean dry towels in the staffroom as it was the most common item of PE kit that students forgot.

I turned the showers off, and handed the towel to the reluctant recipient.

I turned away so that I could give the self conscious lad some privacy, but before I could he whipped the wet towel off – revealing - . . . that he was still resplendent in his soaking wet underpants !

"Oh, son!" I exclaimed for a second time, "Now what are you going to wear to go home in?"

Again the boy looked sheepish, and said nothing.

"Get yourself dried, and bring that towel back to me when you've finished"

By the time the lad had dried and changed I had a letter ready for him to take home to his parents explaining how all lads had to shower after PE, and that I would like them to ensure that he brings swimming trunks for future lessons.

A reply came back from his mother, asking if he could shower at home for the next few weeks and the after that, when he had got used to the other boys, she would provide him with trunks.

This worked. After a month John took part in regular showers. After two months I had to warn him about fooling around in the showers and risking being late for the bell.

Not all boys that are embarrassed changing are first years however, sometimes as the boys reach puberty they become self conscious about the changes in their bodies, and are excused showering or even lessons for a while. The most common of these problems is lads who develop breasts. This hormonal problem normally corrects itself in time, but if it needs a helping hand GP's often prescribe hormone tablets.

Sometimes parents write me a letter explaining the situation, or merely asking for their son to be excused PE for a different reason. Naturally the boys are a bit embarrassed about this anomaly, - but not so Roger Carter. He was a budding entrepreneur. I had to warn him about his behaviour when I caught him charging the other lads ten pence a time to 'have a feel.' The general consensus was 'it was just like the real thing!' But if they were desperate enough to pay, what would these lads know?

*   *   *   *   *

Hawksmount School was not only the best school that I taught in, but also the one in which there were less confrontational kids and also the one that recorded less accidents. Is there a correlation?

There were, however, some incidents. As we e were approaching the end of the winter term the emphasis of the lessons was turning from teaching skills towards putting these skills into practice. I had organised a mini-basketball tournament for one of my fourth year groups. Six teams of five, playing across court, 2 teams on, one resting/refereeing. The team captains came to me, sitting at my recorders desk, at the end of each 15 minute game with their results. Eddie Legg was captain of the blue team, but as it came to his turn to step forward he just stood there and stared at me.

"Come on, Leggy," I said, "what was the score in your game?"

Still he stood there, with a blank glazed look in his eyes. He also seemed to be trembling somewhat. The other boys started to giggle. They thought he was taking the mickey.

Bloody Hell, I thought, *Petit Mal.*- No, not a Del Boy expression but a milder form of epilepsy. Nowhere as severe as the one I encountered at Harry Mac's but still a worry if an incident occurred whilst the sufferer was operating machinery or driving a car.

"Leggy, have you got the results of your match?" I asked again, hoping that he would come out of this episode, but still he stood there shaking.

The kids had stopped giggling and turned quiet as they realised something was wrong.

"OK, captain of the red team, what was the score in your game against Leggy's team?"

"18 – 6, Sir," came red captain's reply.

I turned back to Leggy, hoping to see some reaction. "Is that right Eddie?"

"What, Sir ?" he asked

Thank God, he was back with us.

"The score in your game Leggy. 18 – 6, is that right."

"Yes, Sir."

"Thanks, Leggy."

He hadn't realised that anything had happened.

"OK, change around, Yellow now plays Red, Whites play Skins"

At the end of the lesson I let the rest of the class file out of the sportshall, and pulled Eddie Legg to one side and asked him "Has that ever happened to you before, Eddie ?"

"What, Sir ?"

He still hadn't realised what had gone on, so I explained to him what had happened, and what Petit Mal was. I comforted him with the knowledge that it wasn't a major problem and that he needed to see a doctor to ensure that it didn't develop and cause problems, as it was easily treatable.

"I will need to send a letter home to your parents about this, Eddie. So that they understand. You won't be in trouble over it, don't worry. See me after you've changed."

Ten minutes later, Leggy knocked on my door to receive the letter I had prepared for him to take home. I'd deliberately left the envelope unsealed so that he could see that I wasn't telling his parents anything different to what I'd told him."

Next day, a reply came back from Mrs. Legg. In total contrast to the reaction that I received at Harry Mac's, she thanked me for looking after her son and the advice in my letter. She also informed me that she had made an appointment with her GP.

Another two days later, Mrs Legg once again thanked me but this time the letter informed me that the doctor had given her son medication which he said should totally correct the problem." The letter was accompanied by a bottle of 'Teachers' whisky – *how nice of her to have checked what my favourite tipple was!*

Whilst I was there, Hawksmount School was

also very well respected in the sporting arena, but it wasn't always like that. When I started working there they were only feared at cricket, but Bob and myself worked hard to expand on this.

As you know, I was a rugby specialist but soon realised that this school was better suited for other sports. I coached and ran rugby teams for the first four years of my career there, but eventually concluded that even though we were a large school, (1100 pupils), the same boys were being selected for the rugby teams and football teams on a Saturday morning. Of course we had other boys that could be selected but that would significantly weaken the teams, and nobody likes playing in a sub standard pack that is being crushed by the opposition forwards.

So I abandoned the rugby in favour of Basketball. Bob still ran the football, but our reputation at basketball was poor, even though we had fantastic indoor facilities for the sport.

We also had the best dolomite running track of any school in Cleveland. So, athletics became my summer priority. I took coaching awards in both of these sports and Hawkmount soon became the premier school in the area at both of them, regulary winning Town and County trophies.

Being a rugby player it rankled a lot not to run teams in *my* sport but I still looked out for potential stars to send down to the local rugby club.

We did not, however, end with a whimper.

Just before I ceased running rugby teams, my under 14 and under 16 teams went on a tour of Holland. I got the idea after constantly being bombarded by junk mail from dozens of travel companies that specialised in this field.

After much consideration I (foolishly) chose a company that was not only competitively priced, but whose headquarters were only eight miles away, in Darlington.

I began to fear the worst when this Company, who had a fleet of dozens of coaches, had to hire one in at the last moment.

Thank God Gardiners Coaches of Spennymoor had one available, - even though they had no driver. Also, thank God that this happened - because it meant that the boss, John Gardiner, had to take the job on himself. He did a fantastic job and saved the whole tour from potential disaster.

We were well represented on this trip by high ranking personnel from both of the Companies, as our courier was also the managing director of the Darlington Holiday Company – but, in total contrast, *he was useless.* A total waste of space from start to finish. Not having a coach organised until the last minute was just the start of a catalogue of major errors that he racked up over the ten days of the tour.

It soon became evident that MD had only come along on the trip for a beano, and that his primary interest was not providing a great experience for his paying customers, but rather acquiring as many duty free cigarettes and booze as he could afford. Unfortunately, not many of these duty frees arrived home as he was never at any time seen throughout the tour without a cigarette dangling from his bottom lip, whilst at the same time being permanently sozzled.

The least one should expect from a courier was a good knowledge of the area and a grasp of the language - with MD we got neither. John Gardiner, however, provided both, and throughout the trip saved us on many occasions, even finding us the best places to eat and then negotiating discount prices for providing a large clientelle.

Despite the efforts of MD, we had a really enjoyable tour, and a really successful one too. We left Holland with a 100% unbeaten record, but that was severely put to the test when we played Den Haag. Our lads' jaws dropped when the heavily bearded opposition prop pulled up outside the changing rooms in his own car.

Don't forget the oldest of our boys was 15 years old ! Dopey MD, with his total lack of knowledge of rugby had organised a fixture against their 'Colts' team! Many of their players being 19 y.o.

Fortunately we headed for home with no serious injuries, tired but content with our experience. Now, all that lay ahead for us was the long trek home via Dover. Surely nothing else could possibly go wrong now.

Wrong!

Before boarding the ferry, John announced that we were only making one stop after Dover on the six hour journey home, so now would be a good time to eat and spend our last Guilders on board. So the boys packed out the restaurant and gift shop. - MD went to the bar.

We, stopped at the first service station outside of Dover and the efficient John Gardiner again announced, "Our last stop lads before Ferrybridge. A good time to go to the toilet and phone home *(pre mobile phone days!)* Tell your parents that we will be back in about six hours and that you will give them a definite time from Ferrybridge which will be about an hour and a half away."

The boys noisily crushed off the coach, but not so noisily as to wake MD who was now snoring heavily. John shook him aggressively; I think he was nearing the end of his patience.

"Everybody's phoning home & going to the toilet. Do want to join them?"

"Leave me alone," was all we could make out from the mumblings of MD.

"Sod you" was all that John said.

We both left him and headed for the toilets.

Half a dozen kids had got back on the coach before we returned, and were laughing hysterically as we boarded.

John went to see what the joke was.

"You dirty b****d," he screamed at MD as he shook him roughly, "get off my coach and get your suitcase"

MD stood up to obey the order, and it was then that I saw the dark patch on his light grey trousers. MD had wet himself.

He then had to embarrassingly change into fresh underpants and trousers in the aisle of the coach, before we set off.

"You can shampoo that seat, as well, when we get home. Otherwise my bus will stink."
John's tether *had finally* snapped.

We arrived back at School with no further incidents.

I don't know if John did get his seat shampooed, but I do know that my School never used MD's Company ever again

*   *   *   *   *

The demise of our School's rugby teams was sad, but it did give me more time and opportunities to develop basketball to a reasonable level.

I was already a qualified referee and Teacher/Coach at this sport, but I decided to take my coaching awards to a higher level so attended a Summer school in Sunderland with this objective. I was also a great believer that if you are going to be successful at any venture you need to look the part. If you turn out looking bedraggled, there's a good chance you will produce a bedraggled performance. We didn't have a School basketball strip, and we had no money in the kitty to buy one. So I negotiated with one of our local schools to 'barter' a spare kit off them in exchange for cricket equipment (that we had in abundance).

We ran four teams initially in the school,

from 2nd year to fifth, and enrolled each of them in the Stockton Schools Leagues which we initially struggled in but gradually became VERY successful in over the years.

Success, however, can create its own problems. Running so many teams meant that I had limited time to share out. Bob helped by running the 2nd year team, but now as our initial novices grew older there was demand for a sixth form team. We entered the County Sixth Form league, but matches were few and far between, as there wasn't many other participants. So, I also enrolled them in the Teesside Junior League, which had even fewer participants, but between the two leagues we managed to build up a reasonable fixture list.

This provision was adequate but not ideal, so the following year I decided to ditch these two leagues and take the plunge into better subscribed Men's Teesside BB League.

This would kill two birds with one stone as I was already playing in this League myself for Teesside Schoolmasters, and if I transferred to the newly formed Hawksmount Community College team, I would effectively be saving one night by playing for and coaching the same team.

Even with me in the team and one of the sixth formers, who had now left School, eligible as a Senior, we were still grossly understrength. We were a very successful School team. But we were going to get slaughtered by much more experienced and taller Mens' teams.

So I advertised for players in the local Sports Shop. Just one more experienced player would make a huge difference.

My phone rang first with an enquiry from Steve Williams, an ex First Division forward with YMCA Tigers. Then a doctor who was working at the local hospital who hadn't played much since he was in the England Schoolboys team, and finally Roy Lincoln who had won three National Championship medals with Aldershot Warriors.

Absolutely fantastic, I couldn't have dreamed of such a great response!

Only one problem though, with only five players on court in a ten man team, my sixth formers would be relegated to warming the bench. So I made a 'Club' rule. If we built up a twenty point lead on any of our opponents, we would 'run the bench'

Fortunately this worked! My sixth formers got plenty of court time as we annihilated the majority of teams in the 2nd Division, we gained promotion and won the 'Cambrai' handicap cup that year.

The Handicap Cup win was a great achievement but a little bit unfair on much of our opposition. As the name suggests, each team was given a handicap. Being new boys, and an unknown quantity, we were give a most favourable handicap of 50 points start on the current 1st Division Champions. We met them in the final. They were much better than us but couldn't claw back the fifty points deficit. They hit us with a full court press from the word go which was initially successful but left them tired and very vulnerable in the second half. We eventually beat them by 54 points and didn't need the handicap !

Success, as mentioned above, can create problems, though. We were promoted to Division One and now struggled to beat teams. My sixth formers didn't get many games at all. We were relegated again, pride dented, but problem solved. HCCA Basketball Club became a yoyo team between the two divisions until bad health forced me to quit playing, and the Club folded.

*   *   *   *   *

So, Hawksmount built up a good reputation as a basketball school, we won the County Leagues and Cups on numerous occasions. We even featured in the English Schools Quarter finals on two occasions – both times beaten by London schools; but our most successful sport was Athletics. As an athletics school we achieved much success at National level, twice appearing in the National Schools finals, but disappointingly only becoming the fifth and eighth best school in England on these occasions. We had numerous athletes that competed at Club level in the National Young Athletes League and five that represented English Schools, or better

The first Hawksmount pupil to achieve international level was Guy Henderson, who was selected to hurdle against the French Schools team. Unfortunately he wasn't able to fulfil this commitment.

The next athlete to represent English Schools was Mark Belben, a Long Jumper who finished second in the Home Countries international and so went on to represent GB Schools as well.

By far the most talented at this time, however was Glenn Stephenson, who was selected to train with the GB Junior hurdles squad on account of his outstanding times.

However, hurdles was just one of the ten decathlon events that Glenn was proficient at. He won the 'unofficial' English Schools Championship and his future as an Olympic athlete looked assured. Unfortunately, after attending a GB warm weather training camp in Crete, Glenn took ill. I mistakenly said to him at Athens Airport, as we both were sat with our heads in our hands in the Departure Lounge. "You know, Glenn, that was a great weeks training we had there, but we spoilt it by getting paralytic last night"

I wrongly thought that our 'hangovers' were as a result of the excesses we went through in the last night leaving party. I hadn't realised that we'd both picked up an enterovirus (probably from eating some dodgy food in a local, filthy taverna) and that we were both about to develop serious illnesses.

Glenn died a year later.

Apparently, the virus triggered off leukaemia which was lying dormant in his body, and a very aggressive form of this:- Lymphoma, caused his demise 12 months later.

In my case, the enterovirus developed into M.E. (myalgic encephalomyelitis) which became so troublesome that I had to retire from teaching in 1992, when I was only 41.

Up to that point I was very cavalier in my approach to the food I ate, and associated hygiene. I always thought that my fit body could cope with anything, and that at most I would become bilious or develop diarrohea. Now I am fastidious in all aspects.

Unfortunately, this new awareness came too late to save two promising international careers.

The next international 'athlete' from the school was part of my distance training group, and was as much a credit to his family's influence as was mine. Neil Conway's father, introduced him to the intricacies of Orienteering, and these skills, linked with his undoubted ability as a distance runner resulted in him being selected as Captain of the Great Britain Orienteering team.

Finally, and by far the most successful, of my athletes was Anthony Brannen.

Anth became National Decathlon Champion at both Junior and Senior levels on numerous occasions. He achieved much success at many international tournaments which included a Bronze medal at the 1991 World Student Games, which also resulted in him being selected for the World Championships in Tokyo later that year. Unfortunately, Anth pulled a muscle on the warm up track at these Championships and failed to make the start line. After that Anth's career was dogged with injuries, which included an operation on his throwing arm just before the Barcelona Olympics, and a hernia operation just before the 1996 Atlanta event. After these disappointments Anthony retired, as did his coach !!!

Chapter 5

How Wrong Can One Be ?

Bob Latchford, was great to work with, we got on like a house on fire. Of course we had our disagreements, like any work colleagues do, but it was always resolved in the early days by Bob saying. "Well we are going to do it *my* way. As Head of PE I'll take full responsibility if it is wrong!"

Of course, as a subordinate I fell in line with his decisions, but I'd always let him know that I disagreed, and REALLY let him know if things did go wrong (although Bob will tell you that never happened !)

Later on in my Hawksmount career, Bob moved up to Head of House, in parallel with his PE teaching, and I moved up to Head of PE. We still rarely disagreed about anything, but if we did I always told him . "Well this time we are going to do it *my* way. As Head of PE I'll take full responsibility if it is wrong !"

Bob always gave a wry smile, but knew he just had to take it on the chin.

As you know, I never intended to stay in teaching, but I loved this job so much that I stayed at Hawksmount for 16 years. This was mainly due to my relationship with Bob Latchford, and a great Headmaster, David

Omeroyd (who regularly joked that the worst thing the previous headmaster, George Barton, did was to appoint James Masters, and then promptly leave! – *at least I think he was joking!*).

The kids and the rest of the staff also played a huge part in persuading me to stay

Mind you, as I've quoted in the past, most teachers are boring farts, and I still stand by that, there were only a dozen or so that I would happily go out for a drink with – they know who they are in both cases.

Teachers regularly complain about how little they are paid for the amount of work they do – and they are right. The good teachers work incredibly hard, and *are* underpaid, but it's the deadwood, *boring farts included*, that is holding them (and the kids) back.

As far as I can recall. I had only one occasion in my career that I had a serious run in with one of these farts. He collared me at the end of a staff meeting. The Staffroom was above the Common Room in the sixth form block. As we were all filing out, Bill gabbed my arm. Now it has to be noted that Bill was one of these teachers that arrived at school at one minute to nine in the morning, and already had his last class packed and ready to leave by ten to four at the end of the day.

"Can I have a word?" Bill said, as he brought me to a stop at the top of the stairs.

"Yeah, what's your prob?"

"A few of the staff, are getting pretty fed up with leaving so late from these meetings. If you shut your mouth and stopped all of the inane quips that you make, we could all get home half an hour earlier!"

I couldn't hold back, "Well, unlike some people I don't mind spending extra time to do my job PROPERLY. I'm still regularly here well after the 4 o'clock bell has rung!"

"Well some of us are getting pretty sick of your interruptions and . . ."

"Look Bill," I said devilishly, "I can't argue with you, you are far too intelligent for me, I'm only a thick P.E. teacher - but in the PE department we deal with things like this. . ."

In a flash, my hands were round his throat, as I playfully dangled him over the banister. Then I placed him back on his feet, as I ran away laughing.

Inevitably, next day I was summoned to the headmaster's office.

"Why do you always have to go so far ?" he asked me.

"Why can't you just shrug your shoulders and walk away?"

"Cos he's an ar******" I replied.

"I know, but that's not the way. What if you'd slipped."

"Well I didn't. I was only messing with him." I retorted, "Besides Bill's whole ethic in teaching is to spend as little time doing it as possible. Last one into the car park, first one out every day."

"I know, but can't you just think twice before jumping in feet first every time."

"Yeah, I suppose."

"You owe him an apology."

"I'll take care of it this afternoon – By the way - are you one of the people that Bill referred to, that are sick of my interruptions?"

"NO!" David reacted, "don't ever stop doing it. My meetings are so boring, it's the only thing that keeps most of them awake!"

"Cheers, Boss." I said as I left with a wry smile on my face. Partially, because I had a flashback of Bill's face as I held him over the stairs.

I did write Bill a letter in which I apologised for my actions, I knew they were a bit over the top, BUT I certainly didn't apologise for the sentiments behind my response.

A few months later the Boss promoted me to Head of P.E.

*   *   *   *   *

The main thing that I have to be thankful to Bob Latchford for (and probably what he regrets most) is that he introduced me to the great passion in my life – SKIING.

Bob was the organiser of the annual School's ski trip. He asked me every year if I wanted to go on it, and I had turned him down for four years in a row, claiming that my winter athletics coaching with my group was too important to miss; even for a week.

That *was* partially true, but also I was saving up to buy a house and skiing seemed an added expense that I could do without.

However, on the fifth occasion that Bob asked I replied, "Well I haven't had a holiday for five years. I don't think I'll enjoy skiing, 'cos I can't see the point in strapping a couple of bits of wood to your feet and then sliding down a slope. *Then* going back up and doing it again and again. I bet I'll be bored after the first day! *But* . . . I could do with a holiday, so I'll come along and just mind the kids when you and the other staff need a break."

Latchford just raised an eyebrow, gave a wry smile, and said, "I'm not even going to try to convince you, Just come on the next holiday, and see."

How wrong can anyone be?

I was hooked after three days, and in future years went on every School trip at February half term, after I'd already spent Christmas or New Year skiing myself!!!

When I said above 'I was hooked after three days' don't get me wrong, I loved it from day one, but was addicted after day three !

Just the thrill of meeting at the airport, flying, travelling in a coach from the airport in the valley up the mountain roads, hairpin bends and all, and then the final thrill of entering the 'snow zone' for the first time, pulling up outside of our hotel and unloading suitcases in the snow.

It was all magical, but I still wasn't 'hooked'

until three days in.

This was partly my own fault, because I was so into my sports coaching that I wouldn't give up the occasional session with my basketball teams in order to learn the basics at the local dry ski slope.

Bob told me I was making a mistake, but all I would say was, "Don't worry, I'm a PE teacher, I'll pick it up in no time when we are abroad!"

This was partially right, but I scared the living daylights out of myself (& everybody else around) whilst doing so.

When we arrived for our first morning's skiing, the Head of the Ski School put us in to our teaching groups. My group, obviously, was the bottom 'learners'. Before he took us up the mountain, he wanted to be certain that we could all stop the skis if we got into any difficulty. All the kids went before me as they slid down the gentle slope, executed a perfect snowplough stop, received their praise from Giorgio, and then joined the line waiting to go on the button lift up the mountain.

Then it was my turn. I had watched all of my pupils go before me, and was pretty certain that I had spotted how to do it.

The slope was gentle, so I pushed off a little with my ski poles to gain momentum.

Big mistake !

The speed just got faster . . .and faster . . . and faster. I was hurtling along at more than one hundred miles an hour *(in reality about 5 miles an hour,* but it felt like I was doing the ton).

I tried to push my skis out into the position I'd seen the kids do.

Nothing happened! I just continued gaining speed.

I tried pushing my skis out again. Again nothing happened.

Then fortunately, the slope ran out and started on an upward gradient again, which slowed me down. Giorgio, as all good instructors do, had deliberately selected this area for that very reason. If any novice got into trouble, the up-slope would save them. *He* knew it would stop me – *I thought I was dead !*

Giorgio just took this mishap in his cheery stride. He just gave a big grin, said nothing, slapped me on the back and pointed to the back of the line of kids waiting at the lift station.

I was petrified, I couldn't stop on the gentlest slope in the resort and now this psychopath was taking me on a button lift to the steeper slopes way up the mountain!

Button lifts are the most basic of the uphill travel on the mountains. *I hate them!.*

I did right from day one, I still do. But they are a cost effective way of getting a lot of skiers up a short slope quickly.

So, there I was at the back of this lift queue, the only person in the group that couldn't stop being taken up a half mile long nursery slope, to slide down to my certain death.

All the kids ahead of me kept getting into all sorts of trouble and falling off the lift. All their friends were laughing their heads off.

I was too scared to laugh.

With each one that fell, my eyes just got wider & wider,

Then I felt another slap on my back.

"Jim, drink," was all that Giorgio said, as he thrust a flask of Italian brandy into my hands. I took a huge gulp, smiled and said "Cheers Giorgio" *but I was still not convinced.*

However, being the astute tactician that I was, I had been watching the kids go before me and realised where they were all making the same mistake. There was a bump in the slope about 15 metres after they had started their ascent which caught them by surprise and threw them off the lift. They needed to flex their knees to absorb the bump and then they would glide over it without a problem.

So armed with this information, I took the long metal pole that was handed to me by the lift attendant, shoved the black button on the end between my legs, and squeezed with my thighs to grip it.

Success ! I was moving. Slowly the speed built up, I had gone 5 metres without mishap, then 10, and then 14. Here's the bump, bend the knees, absorb – done it ! I was one of only half a dozen to make it. Brilliant!

I punched the air with my spare hand (the other one holding on for grim life on the metal pole).

Then it dawned on me! I may be one of the few to make it to the top, but I was the only one who couldn't stop. What was I to do when this half mile rope tow ran out ?

Again I turned my attention to studying the people ahead of me to see how they coped.

It all seemed fairly straightforward.

When the lift ended you just took the button from between your legs, threw it into the snow mound at the end, and the slope was banked so that it naturally took you round the corner where you stopped and waited with the rest of the group.

Except I can't stop !

I was panicking but then I realised that all I had to do was grab hold of someone as I met up with the group and that would stop me. Panic over.

Everything went exactly as I planned, I threw the pole away, the slope took me round the corner and I reached out to grab one of the group – only they had already sidestepped out of the way so that people could get past - I missed them.

I hurtled down the half mile slope getting faster and faster. It was like a crevasse, a sheer drop making me go faster with each metre.

50miles an hour, 100, 150, very soon I was breaking the land speed record as I hurtled into oblivion!

In reality the slope wasn't much steeper than my living room carpet, and my speed probably hadn't topped 15 mph. But this was still fast enough to do some serious damage as I flew towards the only tree that stood right in the middle of this green slope.

Should I hit the tree deliberately? Or should I miss it and take my chance that there was a runout slope at the bottom (just like the test area)?

I didn't know, I was rigid with fear.

Then, I saw them:- four lovely girls, Karen, Katy, Diane & Evelyn, from one of the more advanced groups, standing by the tree, having a chat.

I aimed straight for them, grabbed the first one that I came to, and used her to take the other three down like skittles at the bowling alley.

"Sorry, Sorry, Sorry," was all I could say in sheer relief that I was still alive.

The girls were OK about it, no-one was injured. Karen, I think, quite liked it!

After hearing about this near disaster, Bob gave up his dinner hour to take me for a dedicated 1on1 session, in which he attempted to teach me how to stop.

It worked. After this session I caught up with the skill level of the rest of the group and could now save myself without crashing!

Well; not *entirely* true.

The rest of the week contained plenty of crashes, but now of the more humerous kind; where you just lose it on a corner, or whilst you're attempting a new manoeuvre. It is impossible to go through a week's skiing without these incidents. They are things you talk about and laugh about in the bar later. The things that make the trip all that more enjoyable.

There was one other crash and incident, however, that happened to me in this resort, that has never happened anywhere else since.

It was coming to the end of the week, and I had now 'mastered' the nursery slope. Full of confidence, I swished in for a stop at the bottom of the lift station. At the back of the queue, where hundreds of skis had packed down the snow over time; it had now turned into sheet ice.

The ski edges wouldn't grip, and the smile quickly disappeared from my face as my skis went up past my ears and I crashed to the ground with a thump. Next thing, Jenny Ray, one of our female PE staff was picking me up and asking if I was OK.

"Yeah," I said, "no problem"

"Really?" she quizzed, "'Cos you were unconscious there for a couple of minutes. That fella over there," she gestured to a man that was just hauling himself up from his wipeout, "has just skied over your head as you fell."

"Really," I said, "didn't feel a thing !"

"Well you were unconscious for about two minutes. Just shows you how hard your head is!"

To this day, I still don't recollect a thing about it, except that afterwards my arm started hurting considerably and a huge bruise came out of it. It appears that one of this blokes skis hit my right arm and caused painful damage, but the other ski that hit my head caused no discomfort at all.

What is it that they say about PE teachers?

Anyway, despite that accident I had a fantastic, memorable time, and just to add to the experience, at the end of the week I was even awarded a Silver achievement badge at the awards presentation! - (the only downside, *and it still rankles me to this day*, was that Barry, who always came last at cross country and was hopeless at rugby, etc, was awarded a GOLD badge !!!). Latchford never lets me forget!!!

All of the above happened in a wonderful little resort in the Italian Dolomites called Bosco San Giorgio. I will always love this place. I have been on numerous ski trips since, but BSG always holds a special place in my heart, even though on reflection it was a bit of a one horse town. The ski slopes were great for me, plenty of blues and greens, but there was little to satisfy advanced skiers. There was only two hotels in the village – an expensive one and ours (the cheap one) Two drinking holes, a bar that all the instructors frequented and the bar in the expensive hotel. A coffee bar and a sports shop, all built around the village square, and that was it!

Nothing to write home about really, but I loved it !

I think that for anyone who gets hooked on skiing after their first trip (and most people do) their first resort is magical. They've normally never experienced the mountain atmosphere before (which enhances the magic) and have never experienced a sport before that is so thrilling and full of laughs,

If you've never tried it, you must, at least once, before you get too old.

Some people are put off by the expense – but it doesn't need to be much more expensive than the usual beach holiday, if you go about it the right way.

Read www.skiingonashoestring.com on your computer to find out how.

*   *   *   *   *

After becoming addicted in Bosco, I took almost every one of my future holdays on the slopes. I have skied more than two dozen resorts in five different countries, but one of my most memorable trips was when I visited Bulgaria for the second time. This time the skiing wasn't the thing that made it most memorable but the fact that I met Bob's old College mate, Joe Leonard, for the first time.

Pamporovo was a small ski village in the ex-soviet controlled country that was trying desperately to attract western European visitors. Unfortunately, nothing much had changed since its Iron Curtain days. OK, there were a few more luxury items in the shops but it wasn't exactly Harrods. In the old days you could only get Scotch Whisky, perfumed soap, even car tyres, by trading on the black market in hard western currency, but now these things were often, (*not all the time)*, available for the general public to buy. The pound sterling no longer traded to the black marketers at four or five times the bank rate. But, the resort was still great for its prices; not only in the shops, but ski lessons, lift pass and hire of equipment. The skiing on the Rhodope mountains was also quite good, with the famous "Wall" one of the most testing black runs that I have skied.

Joe Leonard, though, was something else.

I met him at Teesside Airport on the way out. He had just returned with Bob from another ski trip in Italy, and he looked haggard. I learned throughout the week that we shared as room-mates, that this was normal for Joe, he always looked haggard.

I decided to greet him on our first morning together with a nice cup of coffee. So, I put on my IRA style, ski mask, you know the type, black balaclava with three holes cut out for the eyes and mouth. Then I put my nose right up to his, and coughed. His eyes blearily opened before he shot out of his skin in rigid fear.

"Morning , Joe," I greeted him, somewhere up near the lampshade, "Do you want a cup of coffee?"

"F*** Off" he croaked through a petrified throat.

"Charming" was my offended reply.

That wasn't the only time we came into conflict. Later on in the week I came in from the skiing, happy but absolutely worn out. All I wanted to do was crash out on my bed for twenty minutes. I would have done that too, if I could have seen my bed for all the garbage that Joe had thrown on it.

He was already asleep on his bed , so I picked everything up and dumped it on top of him. He woke up with a start. "What the . . .?"

"It would be nice to be sleep on my own bed," I snapped at him. "This place is an absolute dump, I hope you're gonna clean it up when you get up !"

Joe went back to sleep but my angry outburst worked. (well almost!)

I don't think 'tidy' or 'coat hanger' were in Joe's vocabulary. All he simply did – under threat from me – was move all of the rubbish to his side of the room. At least his junk was limited now to his space and I had a tidy and tolerable area to my side of the accommodation.

Joe's untidiness and disorganisation didn't end there unfortunately, and almost critically, for him.

On our last day, he asked me "Have you got the tickets?"

"No," I replied, "but thanks for asking. I'll go and get them now from the Hotel safe."

It had been my job to collect all the tickets from the kids as soon as we cleared Customs on arrival, because past experience had taught us that if we left the kids in charge of their own travel documents, there was always one that would lose them. We packed our bags, or in Joe's case; just threw everything off the floor into his luggage and then desperately bounced up and down on the lid hoping to get it closed.

He managed it – just.

"Bloody Hell, why is it that the stuff's so much easier to pack coming out than going home?" he asked surprised.

I couldn't understand why he was surprised at all. "Probably 'cos you got your wife to iron and fold everything. I bet she even packed your case too."

"She did"

"Well there you are then, if you live like such an untidy slob, you shouldn't be surprised that you can't pack things properly. Anyway the lid probably didn't shut 'cos as you swept everything up, you've probably got the litter bin in there too ! "

Joe didn't question this, but he didn't open the case to check either.

When we arrived at Plovdiv Airport the kids all lined up in the Departure Lounge and held their hands out as I called their names out from the tickets. At the end of the distribution there was still one hand still sticking out.

"What?" I asked.

"Where's my ticket?" Joe asked.

"You've got it." I said.

"I asked you in our room if you had the tickets, and you said you were getting them from the safe."

"Yes, you're right," I said, *'the kids'* tickets. I didn't collect any tickets from the adults, they're old enough to look after themselves."

The kids were filing through Passport check,

and the end of the line was getting closer to Joe. With a hint of panic in his voice, he said, "Don't prat about. Just give me the ticket. Joke's over."

"I'm not pratting about, Joe, I didn't collect your ticket."

"Aww Jim," he said, now almost crying, "give me the bloody ticket. It's beyond a joke."

He was now two places off the end of the line, with only myself and Bob to go behind him.

Bob had spotted there was a problem and came storming over. "What's going on? he yelled.

"He's got my ticket and won't give me it." Joe whimpered.

"Give him his ticket, and stop fooling around. We're nearly at the desk"

"I haven't got his ticket. I didn't collect off adults. I didn't collect yours did I. I didn't collect Frank's. Why should I have his ?"

"Just give him his ticket. It's not a joke anymore." Bob shouted with even more venom in his voice."

"Oh, I knew it would be my fault," I protested. "He hasn't been able to look after his equipment all week 'cos he's so bloody disorganised, and now that he loses his ticket it's suddenly all my fault."

Bob could see from my face that I wasn't messing about, he just looked at Joe, shrugged his shoulders and said "I've got the kids to look after, you two sort it out yourselves." He turned, presented his ticket and passport at the desk and went into the next, restricted part, of the Departure Area.

Now this situation would have been bad enough in Britain or the USA or any other Western country, but *this* was Bulgaria; recently an Iron Curtain country, many of whose citizens were desperate to escape to the West. They didn't like anybody trying it on at their airports.

So in my turn, I presented my documents to the desk, looked at Joe, shrugged my shoulders and left.

The last thing I saw of Joe was he was on his knees and begging me not to leave him. This caught the attention of the guard who was at the gate. He walked over, machine gun at the ready, lifted Joe to his feet, and asked him, in Bulgarian for his documents. Joe obviously didn't understand, but replied in English that there had been a mistake and that . . . The guard was having none of it, He roughly bundled Joe into a corner and pointed the machine gun directly at him. The lady who collected the tickets had come round from her desk and was yelling at him in Bulgarian. I felt desperately sorry for Joe, he looked so pathetic and – I've never seen this before – you could actually see the sweat leaving the pores on his bald head and pouring down his face. He was almost crying and his eyes were –pleading with me as I turned and walked into the other room.

Bob was waiting for me. "What the bloody hell is going on ?" He yelled at me accusingly."

"Hey, don't have a go at me," I yelled back,
"I did the job you asked me to do, I collected the tickets from the kids. I didn't collect from any adults !"

"But this is Joe Leonard, he's not an adult. You should have collected from him too!"

I realised he was right, I should have collected from Joe. Up to now he hadn't shown any organisational skills that you would expect from a grown up, but as I'd only just met him, and didn't know at the time of collecting the tickets that he hadn't developed adult skills.

Just then, as we were bickering, Trevor, a teacher from one of the other participating schools walked past. "Hey, you two shouldn't be fighting, we've just had a great weeks skiing and this is no way to end it."

"We're not really fighting," explained Bob, "it's Joe that's the problem," and Bob went on to explain about Joe's missing ticket and the quandary.

"I've got a spare, unused ticket," Trevor unexpectedly announced.

Bob and myself nearly fell through the floor.

"You're joking !" Bob exclaimed.

"No, one of our lads broke his leg playing football on the Saturday before we left. The tickets were already issued, it was too late to take it back."

A huge weight had just been lifted off our shoulders. "Bring it here," Bob said.

Trevor obliged, and when we checked it over it was just the same as ours, except it hadn't been signed in Teesside, and also the top two counterfoils were still intact.

"Hey, you're an Art teacher - do you think you can make it look just the same ?" Bob asked me.

I studied it and said "No problem, the signature is no more than a squiggle. Give me it here."

Everybody huddled round and I stood in the middle of the circle so that the guards couldn't see and when I had forged the signature and removed the counterfoils, I declared "Done, I'll take it to Joe."

"Hey, give me it here" insisted Bob, "You've done enough damage!"

I said nothing, my jaw just dropped. I couldn't believe I was still being blamed for Joe Leonard's disorganisation!

"And don't go telling him it's a forgery until we're home and dry in England," Bob warned, "You know what he's like, he'll panic and give the game away."

Bob disappeared, and came back with a beaming Joe. Everybody was slapping Joe on the back and shaking his hand. He walked past me, called me a b*****d, and continued to the boarding gate.

Onboard, we all settled into our seats and most people tried to get some sleep.

I couldn't sleep, I was too eager to let Joe know his ticket was a forgery, but I'd promised Bob that I wouldn't say anything until we were home. After about an hour, when it was too late for the plane to turn back, my mischievousness got the better of me and I leaned across and whispered "Joe, that ticket was a forgery."

Bob was right Joe panicked and started worrying about Customs & Immigration in England. Bob glared at me. I was able to go happily to sleep, at last.

*   *   *   *   *

Skiing with Hawksmount School was always an epic adventure for me, and I could probably fill a whole book with the incredible accounts of things that I happened to me whilst in the mountains, suffice to say that the next book – Food Parcels to Reading - recounts all of these anecdotes in detail.

Bob Latchford often asks for me to recount the stories when we go for a drink together.

Yes, we still drink together, - and we are still friends, - even though he goes to great lengths to dissociate himself from many of the things that I blame him for.

Chapter 6

What Now ?

It was February 1992, when I was given early retirement from teaching.

I had contracted M.E. but, not really understanding the illness, refused to give in to it.

Of course, since then I have researched it extensively, even to the extent that my specialist told me that I now know more about it than him.

Unfortunately – too late - I realised that my approach had been, up to that point, totally wrong and I had only made the illness worse *and permanent*.

If you are to overcome M.E. you must accept it, and give in to it in the first 18 months of infection, otherwise, like me, you will be stuck with it for the rest of your life.

If this does happen, all is not lost. Even then there are still ways to deal with it.

Initially when I realised I was suffering some sort of illness I just kept working, playing sport and coaching. I did make some concessions, however, by resting (or sleeping) whenever I could and taking paracetomol (normally in the form of Lemsip) four times a day.

When I first went to my GP with symptoms, they took the form of chest infections or throat problems. So, understandably, that was what he treated me for. However, when I kept going back on a regular basis, after not previously seeing a doctor at all for eight years, my GP knew something was seriously wrong.

At first I was tested, for everything possible, in his surgery, then I was sent to hospital for further tests. After approximately two years of monthly tests, my arm was like a pin-cushion, but they couldn't find anything, so my GP came to the conclusion that, as I wasn't a hypochondriac or a skiver, I must have an illness that there was no test for – Myalgic Encephalomyelitis.

To know, what I had, and that I was not going crazy, was a huge weight off my shoulders – but unfortunately it was too late to stop the illness being permanent. However, *now* I could start researching it and treating it.

All this time, as previously explained, I continued to work as a PE teacher. Everyday I exerted my body and made the ME worse. I only stopped training and competing when one day, even though feeling really tired, I drove 5 miles into Stockton to buy a friend a birthday present. I knew exactly what I wanted so I walked directly to the shop from the multi-storey car park – approximately 400 metres. After leaving the store with the gift, I planned to buy some groceries, but was *SO* tired that I crumpled up the shopping list and threw it in a litter bin. It took me twenty minutes to get back to my car. I walked the 200 metres down the centre mall, then tried to climb the stairs to the first level where I'd left it. I stumbled, grabbed hold of the hand-rail and heaved to lift myself up the steps that my legs were failing to negotiate. I stumbled again and heaved again. People walked past and tut – tutted. "The state of him at this time of the morning."

I was too tired to even shout out "I'm not drunk, I'm seriously ill."

So the people kept on passing and tutting, and I kept on stumbling and heaving.

Eventually, after about twenty minutes, I got back to the car. Tears of frustration pouring down my face. It was then it dawned on me - *I should have taken the lift!!!*

Unfortunately, not only was my body extremely tired, but my mind was too. Years of bounding up stairs three at a time had conditioned my brain, as well as my body, into thinking that the elevator wasn't an option for a young man.

However, I no longer felt like a young man, and friends told me I looked older than my Dad.

Nevertheless, I'd made it.

Back at my car, I crawled onto the back seat and slept for half an hour.

When I awoke, I headed for home, but after about two miles I scared myself rigid. I had fallen asleep at the wheel and almost drove into the back of a double decker bus.

I pulled off the road immediately and retook my position on the back seat. This time I slept for twenty minutes before I set off again.

On recommencing the journey, however, this time I only managed another mile and a half before having to park up and sleep again. After another twenty minute nap, I was, fortunately, able to make it back home; all the time spurred on by the thought that I would soon be able to relax properly in my own bed !

Wrong !!!

Once I had arrived home I was too tired to climb the stairs, and this time, with no elevator available, I just crashed out on the settee – and slept a wonderful twelve hours.

This was the most extreme case of tiredness when driving that I had experienced throughout my illness, and although I still drive, I now understand the importance of rest, and I have not, since, come anywhere near to crashing.

Now I always travel with a blanket and a pillow in the boot, and I pull off the road EARLY at the first hint of tiredness.

At home, I also bought a bed/settee and used it regularly downstairs throughout this period. Fortunately, now that I have learned how to MANAGE my illness, I almost always make it upstairs to my more comfortable double bed.

I still drive for good distances, but always plan my route to include a rest period of twenty minutes every hour and a 'back seat' sleep every three.

Last year I drove for a holiday in Ayrshire, Scotland. Google Maps proclaimed that the journey should take three hours at 60 miles an hour. I drove faster – when traffic permitted – but it still took me SIX hours and twenty minutes !

My wife has now become so used to these complications, that she takes a book & crossword puzzles to complete in whatever service station that we have pulled up at. I think over the years she has completed a crossword at every Costa Coffee on every motorway in England.

*   *   *   *   *

When I was given early retirement by Cleveland Education Committee, it was a God-send, but like a fool, and because I was previously hyperactive and a workaholic, I invested my lump-sum into starting my own business.

I had the misguided notion that I could run my own design and printing business, employing other people to do the donkeywork, leaving me to deal with customers; and as a 'second subject' art teacher, deal with any graphics that were necessary. This mistake cost me more than £30k of 'learning the hard way.'

All went well at first, I established the business from home, and employed a friend as secretary/typesetter. Doreen almost ran the business on her own, and I had very little to do.

Even on days when work was slack, she wouldn't - as most other secretaries would do - sit back & read a magazine or file her nails. She would wash up the office crockery, or hoover the carpet. The bonus was that once she got going she was like the proverbial snowball down the hill, and the rest of the house, including the office, became spotless.

Unfortunately Doreen died of cancer at the much too young age of 42.

I was then left in quandary. I needed to employ somebody else to run the business, but I didn't want strangers in my house that I wasn't sure I could trust.

So, I took the big step of renting a premises and interviewing prospective candidates. I knew that there wasn't enough business to afford this but I calculated that I could prop the business up in the short term out of my teacher's pension, and through extensive advertising increase our turnover.

I didn't realise that the short term would last so long.

Over the space of three years I employed five different secretaries, and there was only one good one among them, but I lost her when she was head-hunted by a neighbouring Company.

I was losing money hand over fist and was considering closing the business.

The new secretary that was working for me at that time was taking liberties.

I was trying to run to the schedule that I had set myself:- To open the premises at 8.30 am, and set out the work to be done for that day. Then, to drive out and visit customers on my way home for the dinnertime sleep that was necessary to keep the ME under control. After this, late in the afternoon, to drive back to the office, visiting printers or customers on the way.

This probably would have worked if I had another secretary like Doreen, but Eddie, the current employee just downed tools as soon as I left the office. When I returned he would say that the computer had crashed, and that he had only just managed to get it going again, or the printer wouldn't work, etc. I was on the point of sacking him and closing the business, when fate showed its hand once again.

It was Saturday morning, one of the few when I didn't need to go into the office to finish off a rush job for Monday, so I was enjoying a lie in. The phone rang.

"Is that Mr. Masters? It's Cleveland Police here. Could you come down to your premises? You've had a burglary."

Bloody Hell! No rest for the wicked. I quickly pulled on a tracksuit and headed for Middlesbrough.

When I got to my premises Detective Sergeant Holmes was waiting for me.

"I'm afraid they've taken everything except the desks," he said.

I couldn't believe it, I thought we were burglar-proof. We had bars up at the windows, an anti ram raid post in front of the up & over delivery doors, and a top of the range alarm system. All to no avail, the robbers still broke in through the delivery doors, ignored the alarm going off, ran into the office and picked up the nearest piece of expensive electrical equipment, then ran back out to the waiting van. It was over and done in less than five minutes. They were in such a hurry that they didn't even bother unplugging anything, and as they dashed out, plugs were left in their sockets with a length of snapped cable dangling from them.

The detective merely wanted me to secure the premises, and give him a list of the equipment missing:- two Apple Mac computers, fax machine, photocopier, printer, telephones, etc.

He made his notes and was about to leave when I asked "Do you know, were in the middle of a recession. Businesses are closing all of the time. It's tough going for us, but you haven't once asked me if I did the job myself for the insurance."

"You wouldn't know how to do this, Sir," he explained. "It's a professional job. In fact, it has the hallmarks of just one or two local gangs. If we are quick enough we just might catch them with the stolen goods still on them, but to be honest, I think they'll have fenced them already. . . We'll be in touch."

Of course, they didn't recover the goods. I closed the business, and the insurance money really did come in very welcome.

I told my no good secretary not to turn up from Monday onwards and enjoyed my enforced break.

At last I could put my feet up and just concentrate on the debts that were still owed to me by customers. In the previous few months as the recession seriously took hold, my customer visits had been mainly as a debt collector, I was owed thousands. I had become an expert at taking people through the Small Claims Court. I recovered 80% of the debt, but of the ones that escaped there was one that sticks in my memory.

I regularly received work from Superior Graphics as they specialised in plastic lettering and graphics on vans, shop fronts, etc. My business was paper based: Letterheads, brochures, magazines, etc.

On this particular day, Brian, their proprietor, entered my office: "Hi James, I've got a gentleman here that is setting up a Modelling Agency in Middlesbrough. I've sorted out his signage, but he needs a couple of things that are your department."

"Cheers, Brian." I said, and on that he left to walk back to his premises which were only 100 metres away, whilst I dealt with the customer.

"Yes Sir, how can I help you ?"

The customer was politeness itself, he was well dressed in a smart, light brown suit, but I had to physically stop myself from staring at its left sleeve which was tucked into his pocket. His arm was missing.

"I would like some business cards and letterheads please, and could you also do me some A5 leaflets for a mail drop."

"Yes, that will be no problem" I replied.

He showed me a crumpled piece of paper on which he'd scribbled a rough design. We agreed on typefaces, and graphics and the quantity.

"5000, yes, that will be no problem."

I quoted him the price. He was delighted with it, and immediately started to write out a cheque. I was very surprised, because most businesses needed to be chased for payment after our normal 30 days credit had been over-run. I told him so.

"I know how hard it is to run a business nowadays." He said. "It's all about cashflow. I prefer to pay in advance."

I thanked him sincerely.

Of course, his cheque bounced. I never saw him again.

I walked round to Superior Graphics ten days later, and said to Brian "Do you know that fella with the Modelling Agency? Well his cheque has bounced."

"How much for?" Brian asked

I told him and he retorted "That's nothing, the one he bounced on me was for three times that amount!"

We both decided to call in the Police.

The detective who attended took down the details, but part way through scribbling down, he paused to ask, "Did he have an arm missing?"

"Yes, his left."

"Thought so," the detective replied, "We've been chasing this bloke across the County. He's already pulled off this scam in Hartlepool and Darlington, and we're currently watching a house that he rented. It is full of loaned antiques and paintings, but he hasn't been back to it for four days."

Unsurprisingly, Brian & myself never recovered the money.

Why do people do these things? He didn't get anything out of it except his own perverse amusement.

I suppose it serves to confirm that there are still a lot of sicko's about !!!

*   *   *   *   *

My health suffered badly after the above experiences. My Doctor persuaded me to stop chasing the debts as it was only making my illness worse, and I was once again back on anti-depressants.

I went home and slept – and slept –and slept.

Prior, to catching ME, I was a fit young man. Although I was 37 when ME became troublesome in 1987, and beyond the age when most people retire from competitive sport, I was still playing league basketball, competing in the Northern League at athletics, I had recently taken the Silver medal in the North East Decathlon, and was a workaholic PE teacher.

I was never ill. So it came as a complete shock to me to me to be off work for a long period of time. The first real signs showed on our annual ski trip, when Bob had to carry me off the slopes. To everybody's amusement I had crashed out on an easy corner and couldn't get back to my feet again. The rest of the group thought that I was fooling about as usual, but Bob suspected it was something more serious, but still asked me how much I had had to drink the night before!

He had his fears confirmed when he came to my room twice after skiing to see if I was alright.

He told me later, "I thought it was serious when you came in early from skiing. Then, when I came to your room to see if you were coming to dinner, I was even more concerned when you declined, but later that evening when you refused to come for a drink in the bar; *I knew things were really serious.* You've never ever turned down a drink before!"

When we returned to school, I tried teaching as normal but found things extremely difficult. It even got to the extent where I couldn't stand up for an hour. Lessons in the gym or sportshall were OK, I just sat on a bench, but for outside lessons I had to get one of the kids to carry a chair out for me. I refereed or coached from a sitting position.

Eventually I went to the Doctor's and asked for a tonic or something similar to boost me up as I was feeling tired all the time. I didn't want to be off work, but I knew there was something serious going on. He persuaded me that I needed complete rest and signed me off for a month. One month became two, two became six.

I was obviously concerned that I might have a serious illness, but financially I had no worries. In the teaching profession we were entitled to full wages for 100 days (approx 6 months) when we were on the sick, and this went down to 50% pay for a further 100 days. I'd never been ill for more than two weeks since I caught Scarlet Fever when I was sixteen. So I knew I would be back to work soon.

Still convinced that I couldn't possibly be ill for more than a year, I shrugged off the budgeting that I had to do to make ends meet after six months. However, after 9 months, with no sign of improvement I REALLY became concerned when I was forced to sell my car in order to meet my mortgage payments. The car was brand new – only 10 months old with hardly any mileage on it as I had been in bed most of the time;- but it had to go! It broke my heart to lose £2700 on it in less than a year!

Selling my beautiful brand new Astra was bad enough, but imagine how horrified I was after 12 months when my teachers' sick pay ended and I now had to go onto DSS (now DWP) benefits.

I remember well the conversation with the young lady (using both these words very loosely) from Social Security.

"I think you've made a mistake, you have only sent me a cheque for £168.80."

"That's correct. That is four weeks at £42.20 a week"

"Forty two quid a week!!! I can't possibly survive on that! My mortgage is £350 a month."

"You can't expect us to pay your mortgage for you"

"Well what about all of these people that get their rent for big five bedroomed houses paid by you."

"That's different, they are renting, YOU are buying yours."

"So what am I supposed to do, I can't afford to buy food on this money."

"Well, sell your house"

"SELL MY HOUSE !!! I am seriously ill! The last thing I need is to lose the roof over my head"

"I can't see any alternative"

The next few sentences I said are unprintable, as I punctuated my remarks about paying into National Insurance and never claiming before, and being punished for not being a scrounger, etc., with numerous expletives.

"Sir, if you continue to swear I shall have to put the phone down."

"Put the f****** phone down, you b****," I said as the line went dead.

I was now at the end of my tether. I was *seriously* considering suicide.

So I went to my doctor to discuss my situation and he put me on anti-depressants. They worked wonders. Up to that point I hadn't realised that depression was an illness. I thought that you just needed to tell somebody to snap out of it, and they did (or didn't). But this was definitely something I couldn't snap out of.

After a few months on Amitriptylene, I was once again in fear of having my house repossessed, But this time my brain was in better shape (even if my body wasn't). I decided there was no alternative but to go back to work. I knew I wasn't well enough to do my job properly;- but what alternative did I have ?

M.E. is a weird illness. Initially it doesn't stop you from doing anything, I could still jog out to the football pitches and take a lesson, but it's an accumulative thing. I tired very quickly. If I was able to rest up, or even better – take a nap, between each lesson, I might have lasted longer, but the kids wouldn't let you do that. The best I could do was to sleep every dinnertime. I locked the outside changing room doors, so as not to be disturbed by a knock on our staffroom door, pulled the airbed out that I'd already inflated and jammed behind the lockers, and slept undisturbed for between 20 to 45 minutes. This, plus the fact that normally ME doesn't start to give problems until 72 hours after overdoing it, meant that I lasted three days before I was back on the Lemsips. Then, by taking 4 a day, I managed to survive until the end of the week.

The weekend afforded me a welcome break, and I slept 16 hours a day. But, the writing was on the wall, when after two weeks I had to resort once again to refereeing from the sitting position.

The above techniques meant that I was able to teach continuously for approximately a month before I had to take a couple of days off. Then over the next few months the days off became a more regular feature, until the Headmaster called me into his office.

He was very nice about it, We talked about life in general, before he broached the real reason for the meeting.

"This isn't working, is it, James? You are not doing yourself or the kids any good at all. I'm worried that you are just making bigger problems for your own health."

Then, when I told him about my concerns about losing my house and the 'lady' from Social Security, he suggested that I considered early retirement on health grounds.

I almost somersaulted from my chair with relief.

And so it came to pass.

As you know, I tried disastrously to run my own business which caused a relapse in my ME.

So I decided to find out more about the illness that was so debilitating.

I quickly discovered that the vast majority of the medical profession (my own GP – Dr, Hungin, excepted) knew very little about ME. In fact I also found out when I was still coaching athletics that some were positively hostile towards it.

I had a young Scottish Junior International in my group, who suddenly was struggling with even some of the easier sessions that we were doing. After my own experiences, I was almost psychotic that she didn't train too hard and develop ME, so I told her my concerns. She agreed to see a doctor, but being a university student in her first year, and away from home, she didn't have a car and didn't know where the GP's surgery was that the Uni. had arranged. So I agreed to escort her.

When I told the doctor my worries about hard training and ME, he retorted "No such thing as ME. It's all in the mind."

I almost blew a fuse, my face went purple, but my priority was to get Anne treated, so I bit my tongue.

After getting home I wrote this doctor a very stern letter, pointing out that I was an International Athletics Coach who had had my coaching restricted due to contracting ME. I also told him that it was commonly accepted, amongst researchers, that nobody had ever died from contacting ME – but at least five had committed suicide through lack of support from their GP. I hoped that he wouldn't cause an increase in this number through his ignorance."

I didn't receive a reply!

Chapter 7

The Hereafter

Throughout the period that I was badly ill with ME, I kept my coaching group going at Clairville Stadium in Middlesbrough.I discussed schedules with Paul, my Assistant Coach (who later became a skilled coach in his own right), and he conducted them. Most of my senior athletes were able to look after themselves for 90% of their schedules. So things trundled along nicely. Not ideal, but I always thought that one day I was going to be able to pick up where I left off.

I occasionally got down to the Stadium on 'good days' to observe and advise. The athletes all knew that I was on the end of the phone if they ever needed to talk over any problems they had.

I never did get back into the coaching that I loved.

This book concentrates on my teaching experiences, but the next one contains some hilarious stories of things that you wouldn't believe could happen (to anyone else but me) when on International duty. Like the Warm Weather training camp, at which I had to hitch a lift, with sixteen foot vaulting poles, from the only Cockney ice cream man in Portugal, or the punch up that I almost had with the Polish coach who stole our javelin in the middle of a Decathlon in Fielderstadt, or the German ex P.O.W, that I met at the World Student Games in Duisburg, who loved life so much as a prisoner that he didn't want to go home when the war ended.

*   *   *   *   *

Unfortunately, I had to give up coaching in order to successfully 'manage' my illness. I know there are still days when I could successfully coach, just like there are days when I could successfully hold down a job, but it is all about not taking on more than I can cope with. I can't commit to anything that involves regular attendance, because just as there are 'good days' when I can take on the world, there are also bad days when I need to spend most of it in bed. The more I take on during the good days the more bad days I experience.

So I have to 'manage' the illness, and I do this by:

a) **Pacing** – attempting projects in small, easy to manage segments

b) **Sleep** - when feeling tired (or complete rest if that's not possible)

c) **Avoidance** – of any triggers that set my ME off.
This could be physical or mental stress, allergens, or even germs

and infections that other people carry.

It is virtually impossible to avoid all of these so consequently I suffer bouts of ME on regular occasions. However by following the above 'coping strategy' it is possible to reduce the number and length & strength of relapses, and to live a relatively 'ordinary' lifestyle.

The above strategy is not just a system that I have conjured up myself but the accumulation of research and advice given to me by various doctors & organisations.

I could go deeper into this, but it would only bore the readers that have no interest at all in it – so if you need to know more, look up the Further Reading section at the end.

Life can be lived relatively normally, if I am careful, but some things that other people would consider normal have to be attempted with caution. For example, holidays:- the extra walking, sightseeing, & disruption to my sleep patterns, often mean a three week or more relapse when I return home.

Many other things, however, can be enjoyed as normal, I enjoy going to football matches, although nowadays I mainly watch on TV and I enjoy a pint in the pub - but even a humdrum lifestyle like this can create unexpected escapades.

One night, Bob and myself were enjoying a pint on our local pub, when an ex-pupil of Hawksmount walked over and said " I hope that you are both coming to next week's Reunion at the Turk's Head."

"Don't know anything about it," I said. "We're probably not invited"

"I'm inviting you now," she replied.

"Well, I can't make it," Bob added, "I'm visiting Joe in the States next week."

"I hope you can still come, Mr. Masters."

"I'm not sure, you know, if I don't have my body guard with me . . . who else's going ?"

"Well, there be all the lads from the football team. They said they're going:- Porky, Maccas, Ginner, you know . . ."

"OK, sounds good, I'll put it in my diary, and try to make it"

So, a week later, I entered the Turk's Head with trepidation (Bob couldn't come!) and immediately located the footballers, propping up the bar. Deep into a conversation with Porky, I glanced over his shoulder and sitting, on her own, by the far wall was a gorgeous red-head, who I thought I recognised. She was staring straight back at me and smiling.

I looked around to see who else she might be looking at, but they were all in deep conversation with each other. So I glanced back across at her, and again she looked back and smiled.

Yep, it was definitely me that she was paying attention to. So, I smiled back again, and began to puzzle.

I definitely recognised her, but who was she?

As a PE teacher I only taught boys, but I did coach a girls basketball team I'm sure, if she'd been one of them, I would have recognised her.

Of course, she could be one of the girls athletics team, because we did have mixed matches in the summer. Maybe that's where I know her from.

I glanced back again, yeah, that was probably it, because with legs like those she could definitely be an athlete – a high jumper, most likely.

Her legs seemed to go on endlessly. They protruded out from a denim dress that was split to her waist. The top of the dress was *very* low cut. She had a fine pair of boobs that precariously clung to the inside of the denim. I was sure that if she coughed one would drop out.

I had the serving spoon warmed & ready.

Everything was topped off with long flowing auburn hair that hung down over her shoulders and framed her beautiful tanned, smiling face.

As she was sitting on a direct route to the Gents, I took the opportunity to chat to her as I returned from a visit.

"OK then," I said, "You keep smiling over, and obviously recognise me, but you have me at a disadvantage, 'cos although I recognise you, I can't recall your name."

"You know me very well," she said, " you used to laugh at me in lessons when I couldn't kick the ball straight."

"Ah, that's where you're mistaken. It was Mr. Latchford who took girls' football. I was the rugby man."

She wouldn't have it.

"No, it was definitely you, you also used to take the mickey because I wasn't very good at running as well."

"Well, I think you're mistaken, but, whatever, it doesn't matter. What's your name then?"

She gave another of her big, beaming smiles, and said, "Well, I don't know whether to tell you my name now, or wait until tomorrow morning and tell you in bed when we wake up."

I nearly dropped my pint.

"Well, the last option is out of the question, - I'm happily married. So, let's just go with option number one, and you tell me your name straight away."

"Anthony Dalton" he said.

This time I put my glass down on the table, 'cos I was sure either it, or me, was going to fall.

"Anthony Dalton," I gasped, jaw dropped, *"Anthony Dalton?"*

"Bloody Hell, Tony!" I looked her up and down once again, "You make a much better woman than you did a man!

I turned and looked around the bar. They were all in hysterics. They all knew. I was the only one that didn't.

Amazed and intrigued, I turned back to

him/her and asked, "Is it all you then?
Or is most of it false?"

"No it's all me, I had hormone treatment
for the boobs and grew and dyed my hair. The
eyelashes are the only false part."

Even more inquisitive, I pried "What about
down below then, are you still a man there?"

"No, I had an operation about four years
ago. I'm all woman."

"And does it all work like a woman?"

"Yes, just like a normal woman!"

"Have you tested it out?"

"You bet," she replied. "It took me about
nine months to recover fully from the operation,
and then I took a holiday in Majorca to
celebrate. I had everybody in the hotel from the
bell hop to the front desk clerk."

"Jeez ! Did you tell them you'd been a
man?"

"No, I definitely didn't!" she exclaimed.

"Good move," I blurted, "'Cos I think if you
had, you'd have ended up back in hospital pretty
damn quick !"

*   *   *   *   *

Despite having ME, I, occasionally, test
myself out and try to push the boundaries.
By experimenting I have found that I can no
longer play a full game of golf, but I can cope
with the driving range. If I tried to walk around
18 holes it would leave me ill for weeks. Just to
walk from tee to pin in a straight line, is more

than four miles, but the way I play, zig-zagging down the course, it would be closer to ten miles.

That would have tested me even as a young man. I hated walking, I used to run everywhere.

Now, look at me. I can't even walk a NINE hole course without repercussions. As already mentioned I can hit 20 balls on the driving range no problem, but 50 balls makes me ill. That probably means I could walk & play just three holes. So, what's the point?

Consequently, I sold my clubs.

I wasn't much good at golf anyway. I don't miss it that much.

The sport that I really miss however is skiing.

Not just for the thrill of going fast downhill, but also for the scenery, the mountain environment, the fresh, clean air, camararderie and après-ski.

It would probably be a great holiday just to experience these aspects alone, even without the skiing. I used to think of doing just this, but in reality, it was all just daydreaming, because on my finances it would be far too expensive.

Imagine my surprise then, when a rich friend of mine offered to pay for me to go with him - if I arranged *everything* and taught him to ski.

With little thought for the consequences, I jumped at the chance.

So, Doug and I set off for Rauris in Austria.

We had agreed that he would be in lessons every morning and I would watch him on the nursery slopes in the afternoon & take photographs.

This all sounded *SO* easy; I knew it couldn't possibly cause a relapse of my illness.

In fact, my illness would probably improve because of the mountain air and the psychological lift to my spirits.

But, as the saying goes:- all the best laid plans . . .

Our gasthaus was 400 metres from the ski schule, so that was an 800 metre round trip (half uphill) even before using more energy at the slopes!

I took Doug to lessons on the first day, just to ensure that everything went OK and I arranged to meet him again at 1pm. I took a few photographs and then went back to the gasthaus to sleep.

I rendezvouzed with Doug, as arranged, and we had a snack for dinner – Rotwurst (my favourite!) and chips, washed down with a pint of Bavarian ale.

Then after being sufficiently rested and sated, we went back to the nursery slope where Doug practiced what he had done in that morning's lesson. I could see he wasn't happy so I consoled him with "You know, this is the hardest part, Doug. Once you have mastered how to stop and turn, they'll take you up the mountain, and you can say bye bye to the nursery slopes."

"I don't mind the nursery slopes," he said, "it's all this bloody side stepping up and down, just to get a ten metre run. It's exhausting, and frustrating. I thought we'd be going up in chair lifts."

I told Doug about my experience in Bosco where I nearly killed myself by going up a lift and not being able to stop, and this put a smile on his face. He attacked the side-stepping and snow ploughing now with more vigour.

"You know, everybody experiences this when they first learn, Doug," I reassured, "but you'll probably be on that rope tow tomorrow, and things will get a lot easier."

Doug looked at me and gave what can only be described as a half grimace, half smile.

We went for another Bavarian pint, after this, in our 'local' at the bottom of the slopes and then dragged ourselves back to our lodgings, where we both crashed onto our beds and I slept for the second time that day – almost missing dinner – which would have been a pity as the home-cooked Austrian cuisine in our hotel was gorgeous.

The next day was a repeat of day one and when I met up with Doug he was fuming "What a bloody waste of time. The instructor said I was ready to go on the lift, but I can't 'cos the whole group has got to go up together, and there are some w*****s who are not ready yet. Can't you take me up ?"

"Not really, Doug, first of all I don't have a lift pass or ski's. Secondly, there would be all sorts of insurance implications if you had an accident."

"Well, OK," he said, "but I'm not doing any

more bloody side stepping today, I've had my fill. Let's go for a pint."

That suited me – I moved on with an extra spring in my step, until he said "By the way, it's your round."

That night after dinner and our now usual afternoon kip, we felt energised and went out on the 'town'. Rauris is only a medium sizes ski village, with a handful of bars and restaurants, so we soon found the liveliest of these, "Shakes Beers," as you could hear the noise, coming from it, half way down the main street.

We had a couple of bierres in there, but when Doug was keen for a third, I cautioned him that he'd come here to learn to ski, and a hangover and leaden legs would make progress even slower; meaning he'll forever be on the nursery slope.

Reluctantly, but wisely, he decided I was right, and we both took an early night.

The next day, Doug was much happier, they were now using the lift on the nursery slope, and he was skiing down, *in stages*, the quarter mile slope.

" The instructor told me that he'll move the slow learners into a lower group,and tomorrow we're going up the mountain," he beamed.

I knew that this was where my problems started, 'cos if Doug went up the mountain, I had to go up the mountain too! And if I was to teach him, as we had arranged, I would have to ski down with him.

Unchartered territory for me, but as Doug

was a learner, the slopes he would be sking on should be easy for me, so not too stressful.

Wrong !!!

That night we went to ShakesBeers again, and discovered just why it was so lively.

We met a couple of squadies who told us that the British Army Telemark Championships were in town.

Now ShakesBeers Bar is normally the liveliest in the village but this week it was rockin'! These squadies were already steamin' – and it was only early. It was frightening to think of what sort of state they would be in at closing time.

Next Day, Doug appreciated my advice of not getting intoxicated on the previous evening, because the ski instructor, true to his word, took the group up the mountain – *and it was frightening.*

Rauris is a lovely little Austrian resort, I loved everything about it except this. The progression from easy nursery slopes to the blue slopes was too big a step and too scary for some of the group. In most Alpine countries these slopes would have been graded red rather than blue, and the immediate effect was that two of the less confident members of the group dropped out and asked to be put back into the lower group. Unfortunately for me, Doug was not one of them.

So on this day our lunchtime meet was at the restaurant, half way up the mountain.

I set out to meet Doug an hour earlier than

usual, because I had to hire some skis and purchase a lift ticket. I met him outside of a beautiful, pine, chalet-style mountain restaurant.

Quite simply the best I've been to anywhere in the Alps.

The food was varied and good; not too pricey considering its location, but best of all, they had a live rock band, playing sixties music all lunchtime. Where else? ? ?

I didn't want to leave the restaurant, but Doug insisted. All lunchtime he had been telling me how wonderful it was on these slopes 'up the mountain'. This was real skiing. He loved it.

What a difference a day makes!

Doug recounted all the crashes that the group had had on these steep and scary slopes, and how everything was made much harder as now they were hurtling along.

I took him over everything they had done that morning, on the same slopes, and to be honest we travelled at a snail's pace. It was still fast for a novice who only had very gentle nursery slopes to compare to, but I had to agree with him on the other point; for beginners, these slopes were *scary!*

I've generally skied black slopes and off-piste in the past, so I knew that I was more than capable of doing this – especially at the pace we were moving – but in the past, I didn't have ME, so I didn't know how my body and legs were going to cope.

As it happens, I skied fine. Doug wound his

way slowly down the piste making lots of turns, whilst I coached and took loads of photographs.

Then I skied past him, in a direct line which was less tiring on the legs, and watched him come towards me for the next twenty metres.

And so it went on, until before we knew it we were standing outside the restaurant, two miles down the mountain.

"That was great !," Doug enthused. "Much better and much faster than this morning."

Much faster ? I couldn't believe it, the sides of my feet were aching from standing still with them dug into the side of the mountain to avoid slipping.

"Let's go again !" Doug yelled.

I wasn't so keen. "We might not have enough time before the lifts shut," I warned, "and then we would have to ski right down to the bottom of the mountain, and you're not up to it."

"We'll be alright, I'll ski faster." Doug shouted back, already half way to the bubble lift.

This was what I'd feared, I was starting to tire and in danger of triggering my ME, but Doug had paid for me to come, so I couldn't refuse.

He did say he would ski faster, and true to his word he did. I don't know if we made any better time, 'cos faster also meant three times more crashes – but Doug loved these too. He was hooked.

I was loving it too – but worried about my legs that were now burning and throbbing.

Fortunately, we made it for the last lift down the mountain, and by the time we had our usual pint (or was it two?) in our local (which was literally a 15 metre downhill walk from the lift station) I was feeling OK.

Our gasthaus was only 400 metres walk from there and the first 100 metres were downhill to the bridge across the river, but then the next three hundred went up the other side of the valley and now my legs were really dragging.

After dinner that night, Doug went to ShakesBeers on his own, I'd had it: and was asleep by 10 pm. – I don't know what time Doug rolled in – but roll was the operative word.

Next morning, at breakfast Doug looked haggard. I didn't look or feel much better, but *his* was self-inflicted. Still he couldn't wait to tell me about his night.

"Do you remember those squaddies we talked to ?"

"Yeah."

"Well, last night one of them told me that he had competed in the Telemark Downhill yesterday at 9 am, but that he didn't get in from the Bar until 5.45 am. He only had time to shower and eat breakfast before he had to go up the mountain to register."

"And ?"

"Well, he was third person on – but crashed out at the first gate. His legs were so drunk that he couldn't turn !"

Well, what a waste." I commented, "He

came here to compete and got so drunk that he ruined his chances. He could get drunk any night of the week – at home!"

"He wasn't bothered" Doug replied. " Like he said, he'd got a week off duties, got drunk on really cheap beer, and the Army paid half the cost of his trip !"

"Well, I suppose if that's your sole interest in life. I hope he's happy – I wouldn't be."

"No, neither was his Commanding Officer.

He's given him two weeks in the glasshouse when they return to barracks ! But still, he thinks it was worth it !!!"

*   *   *   *   *

By the end of the week, Doug had conquered these slopes and looking back was really pleased at what he had achieved. So was I, these were challenging slopes and he had done exceptionally well. From now on it would be plain sailing for him at *any* resort.

As for me, I won't be skiing again. I was glad I tried and found out that it was too much for me. From mid-week (at the time the above incident occurred) I was having to hit the pain killers at maximum dosage, and strap up both knees heavily. I knew I was 'borrowing' energy that I would have to pay for when I returned home. Still, I was pleased I did it, even though it caused a massive relapse, and I spent the best part of the next three months fighting off the after effects of the over-exertion.

Would I do it again ?
Maybe, if it was free, I would be tempted again: - otherwise definitely (maybe) not.

*   *   *   *   *

So, that was more or less my life in full time teaching.

The next book – "Food Parcels to Reading" – covers my life outside of teaching, which was even more eventful !!!

Further Reading

Also by James Masters

Food Parcels To Reading
(Out Now on Kindle & in the Amazon Store in Paperback)
As I jotted down initial notes for this book, "Fated . . .", I quickly realised that I had far too many stories to tell and that they would make the book unwieldy. So, the content was split.

F.P.R tells of my escapades, mainly outside of teaching, from birth in a rough area of Middlesbrough to my present, happy retirement.

Working in Sport (3 editions) by How To Books
Ever fancied a job in Sport but didn't want to teach or join the Army?

Information on how to get a sports related job whatever your level of skill.

Skiing on a Shoestring.com
Website of the day on Radio Two, uncovers how to go skiing (whether first time or experienced) much cheaper than you thought possible.

More Information about
Myalgic Encephalomyelitis (M.E.)

http://www.investinme.org
www.meassociation.org.uk

Dr. Jay A. Goldstein is director of the Chronic Fatigue Syndrome Institute of Orange, California. His background as a medical doctor is in psychiatry and family practice, but for a number of years now, he has specialised in the care of CFS/M.E. and related disorders.
Goldstein has lectured and written extensively on this topic, including his latest book, Betrayal of the Brain.
To help explain his approach in layman's terms, Katie Courmel has written the book "A Companion Volume to Dr. Jay A. Goldstein's Betrayal of the Brain."
In the United States Myalgic Encephalomyelitis is often referred to as CFS (Chronic Fatigue Syndrome). Many physicians are lobbying to have this changed to the terminology used in the UK, which they consider more descriptive.

Books by Dr.Goldstein:-
Chronic Fatigue Syndrome: The Struggle for Health (1990)
Could Your Doctor Be Wrong? (1991)
Chronic Fatigue Syndromes: The Limbic Hypothesis (1993)
Betrayal By The Brain: The Neurologic Basis of Chronic Fatigue Syndrome, Fibromyalgia Syndrome, and Related Neural Network Disorders (1996)
Tuning the Brain: Principles and Practice of Neurosomatic Medicine (2004)

Professor Julia Newton "What is ME?" – useful booklet intended for solicitors